Promoting Assessment as Learning

Promoting Assessment As Learning sets out to re-examine the relationship between assessment and learning in the classroom. It argues that assessment is an important part of pupil learning, and needs to be understood by pupils in order to help them make judgements about their own progress.

This timely book explores theories of learning and assessment within the context of national tests and also through the theme of self-assessment. It offers practical approaches to help teachers translate national policy into meaningful classroom practice, and suggests ways to help pupils develop their own assessment skills through a process of consolidation, reflection and revision.

This book will appeal to new and practising primary school teachers and headteachers and those on in-service courses. It will also be of interest to students on initial teacher training and higher degree courses.

Ruth Dann lectures in Primary Education at Keele University. She is also the Deputy Editor of the journal *Education 3–13*.

For Mum and Dad

Promoting Assessment as Learning

Improving the Learning Process

Ruth Dann

London and New York

First published 2002 by RoutledgeFalmer
11 New Fetter Lane, London EC4P 4EE

Simultaneously published in the USA and Canada
by RoutledgeFalmer
29 West 35th Street, New York, NY 10001

RoutledgeFalmer is an imprint of the Taylor & Francis Group

© 2002 Ruth Dann

Typeset in Sabon by
Keystroke, Jacaranda Lodge, Wolverhampton
Printed and bound in Great Britain by
TJ International Ltd, Padstow, Cornwall

British Library Cataloguing in Publication Data
A catalogue record for this book is available from the British Library

Library of Congress Cataloging in Publication Data
Dann, Ruth.
   Promoting assessment as learning : improving the learning
   process / Ruth Dann.
      p. cm.
   Includes bibliographical references (p.) and index.
   1. Educational tests and measurements—Great Britain.
   2. Examinations—Great Britain. 3. Learning—Great Britain. I. Title.
   LB3056.G7 D26 2002
   372.126'0941—dc21   2001048581

ISBN 0–415–24006–9 (hbk)
ISBN 0–415–24007–7 (pbk)

Contents

Figures

Acknowledgements

Inspiration for my work in assessment was triggered by my PhD work with Roger Murphy in the late 1980s at Southampton University. My continued interest and concern has been through contact with many teachers, pupils and intending teachers during my time teaching at Highfield Primary School, Southampton, and lecturing at Keele University. My thanks go to all who have in some small way sparked my thinking. Specific thanks go to Colin Richards who dared to suggest that I write a book, and for his constructive comments on an early proposal. Particular thanks go to my father who has tirelessly read early drafts and proofread the text. Finally to my husband, Mark, who has encouraged me throughout.

To protect their identity the names of schools and participants have been changed in this book.

Abbreviations

DES	Department of Education and Science
DfEE	Department for Education and Employment
KS	Key Stage
NC	National Curriculum
PACE	Primary Assessment, Curriculum and Experience
PGCE	Post Graduate Certificate in Education
QCA	Qualifications and Curriculum Authority
SATs	Standard Assessment Tasks
SCAA	School Curriculum and Assessment Authority
SEAC	Schools Examination and Assessment Council
STs	Standard Tests
TGAT	Task Group for Assessment and Testing
TTA	Teacher Training Agency

Chapter 1

Introduction

'Can you light a fire?'

(Teacher Training Agency 2001)

Any teacher who has survived a decade of educational reform may well respond with 'give me a chance' or 'yes – inspite of the superfluous documentation'. The focus of the Teacher Training Agency's (TTA) invitation to a career in teaching surely strikes a chord with many in the profession whose central aim is echoed in this challenge. Its underlying argument is a powerful one. It catches completely the insight that the overarching task of the teacher is to excite pupils in the complex world of learning – lifelong learning. It gives proper recognition to the truth that, far from being receptacles for the insertion of tightly prepacked knowledge, children are active participants in authentic learning. Unless the fire be lit in the mind and spirit of the growing child, whatever the outcome, it will be something less than that promised in such a learning experience. The quest for genuine learning, however, demands a commitment far removed from sentiment. It can never forsake the pursuit of clarity and precision. It cannot be content with vague feeling or undue indulgent emotion. If the child's mind is to be sharpened, his will challenged, his interest aroused and his whole being engaged in the course of construction and discovery, an evocative *flint* is essential.

Certainly, concern with educational standards fired national reform. A National Curriculum accompanied by national assessments now seeks to ensure that school provision is suitably surveyed, and commensurate with national needs. It is hardly surprising, then, that assessment issues and practices have featured prominently since the passing of the Education Reform Act, 1988. The involvement of teachers in piloting, monitoring, reviewing, implementing, marking and moderating has been cast in a rapidly changing, and often confusing, context. Understandably, their responses to the demands of national assessments have been varied. Some sensing a depreciation of the credibility of their own judgements, and an unacceptable marginalisation of their role have succumbed to dismay, if not to the boycotting of all involvement with national tests. Others there be who have sought to cooperate with the new demands and have assumed massive powers of interpretation in transforming their practice in line with the new and changing national agendas.

Emerging from what seems like a deluge of policy developments, are clearly defined testing requirements. These, it can be argued have led to the development of a testing culture in schools, even in the primary phase (Chapter 4). Accordingly, teachers may well wish to 'turn down the heat' as the pressures of change bear greatly on expectations of them and their pupils. But another view may be construed similarly. Hence, the way in which learning is conceptualised and related to assessment requires some attention. There is very little attempt within the prolific documentation since 1988 to tease out how pupils learn. Implicit in the strategies and policies promoted are glimpses of a rationale or a perspective which is inarticulated and unchallenged. Trying to relate what is embedded in current policy and practice to the broader field of education and learning is one part of the focus of this book (Chapter 2). Furthermore, there is an attempt to promote a particular view of learning with implications for assessment. Indeed the implications for assessment are such that they call for a reappraisal of assessment as a concept. Additionally, implications are raised for assessment practices as the relationships involved in learning, assessment and teaching are re-examined.

Fundamental to the argument advanced is the idea that learning, ultimately, is constructed and controlled by pupils. Without teachers' willingness to engage with the curriculum and pupils' developing range of cognitive competencies and experiences, learning will not proceed. If assessment genuinely seeks to give some indication of pupils' levels of learning and development, in ways which will further advance learning, pupils will need to understand and contribute to the process.

Also at stake is the way in which pupils make sense of the testing climates and practices around them. Fears that some National Curriculum tests do no more than suspend the curriculum and interrupt 'real' learning are not supported here – in such simplistic terms. Children and teachers have the capacity to transform any educational encounter into a valuable learning experience. Even national tests can be a source of learning! An example is offered by way of illustration for this assertion. It is anecdotal and possibly untypical, but it is real and serves as an introduction to possible ways in which learning and assessment may be viewed.

It was the middle of May, a time marked in primary schools up and down the nation by national standard tests. We visited some friends for the evening. Our arrival was specifically timed to ensure that all children were tucked up in bed for the night. It marked the week when Daniel, the son of our friends, had been undertaking his Key Stage 1 reading tests. They relayed the following to us, as (sadly) they thought I might be interested. Daniel had come home from school the day before in a quandary. 'I don't know which coloured diamonds are *the best*', he said. 'It could be the red ones, or the blue ones, or the yellow ones. There are lots of coloured diamonds – did you know?' His parents confessed to him (and to us) that they did not know there were many colours of diamonds. Daniel proceeded to rehearse some of the virtues of diamonds. By this time the whole family were intrigued. But what Daniel could not decide was what colour was best. Indeed the Key Stage 1 reading comprehensive test (level 3) which he had taken that day included a small colour pamphlet with a range of information about diamonds, their origin and the uses. It illustrated the different colours available and their relative rarities. But the booklet did not give the information to answer *his* question – which was the best. (This was not one of the questions asked in the test.) Daniel was reported to have muttered his thinking on this for some time, as he changed his mind from one colour to another. I am not sure of the reasoning behind his wanting to make the decision about choosing the best colour diamond, for possible future events perhaps! What was clear was that the reading test had provided a source of information which had engaged Daniel. He was asking questions, thinking deeply, reviewing ideas and facts, telling others, asking others and involving his whole family. He was most certainly learning. How well he did on the test I do not know at the time of writing – I suspect rather well! He had translated the test into a learning opportunity. On this occasion, the distinction between assessment and learning seemed somewhat blurred in the reality of the classroom and for the individual pupil. Of course when the results are listed and the levels promoted, the whole process of learning which Daniel embarked upon will not be evident.

The aims of this book are fourfold. First, it seeks to promote an understanding of learning that can underpin teaching and assessment within education, particularly but not exclusively primary education. The emphasis here is on constructivism and the fundamental view that pupils construct their own means from the experiences around them. Second, it examines the context of Year 6, characterised by the demands of end of Key Stage 2 national tests. From this context, the way in which test preparation can contribute to, rather than hinder learning, is considered. Third, from the perspective of promoting learning, pupils' own role in the process is outlined. This includes their involvement in the assessment process as part of their learning progress. Finally, it aims to set the ideas of assessment and learning which it promotes within a framework of teacher professional development. This seeks to recognise the role and responsibilities of teachers in shaping and facilitating pupil learning, within a national educational context.

In pursuing these four strands, the book seeks to extend some of the theoretical insights underpinning assessment and learning, particularly in the areas of self-assessment and Year 6 teaching. The content is informed by some small-scale research initiatives, but they are not presented as a full account of research methodology. Much of the work presented requires further substantial and sustained research. They are offered in a context which is developmental and in need of considerable research effort at both national and international levels. Whilst intended to be significant the contribution offered here in no way claims to be exhaustive.

The text is not intended as a practical guide, although it does seek to promote, inform and guide practice: practice which is more strongly informed by the principles of learning and seeks to reconsider the relationships between teaching, learning and assessment. The ideas developed are sensitive to context and the competing demands which bear on classroom realities. They pose a considerable challenge, requiring teachers to make sense of a national educational context in ways which are not frequently promoted. These ways, on the surface, seem to suggest incompatibilities and diversity. Perhaps the message from the TTA to 'light a fire' offers us more of a clue than was intended for teachers. Surely, lighting a fire usually needs some form of friction in order to gain the spark. Although what is offered here is not intended to cause sparks to fly, it will not sit comfortably for some! Inevitably there will be friction as different ideologies are compared and a particular argument is promoted. This book offers a genuine endeavour to 'raise the temperature' of children's learning.

Specifically the chronology of the book is outlined as follows. Chapter 2 explores the ways in which pupil learning is assumed to develop within the context of National Curriculum and assessment arrangements. It seeks to make explicit that which, in relation to learning development, remains implicit in assessment and curriculum directives and policies. The role of the learner is examined in relation to the demands of contemporary curriculum requirements. Additionally, the 'products' which are promoted and assessed are viewed in relation to their emphases in learning. This discussion is contextualised in both the rhetoric and realities of the learning society, the economy and its needs and the promotion of particular cultural priorities. The analysis is policy based. By contrast an alternative view is explored which seeks to focus on process rather than product and which recognises the fundamental centrality of the pupil as learner. It rests on the view that learning is socially constructed. The chapter sets up a tension between the view of learning apparent in national policy and that which seems to make sense in terms of understanding the process of pupil learning. The endeavour to go some way towards reconciling these tensions provides the focus for the remainder of the book, as processes of assessment are explored in ways which may serve as sources learning.

In further examining the way that learning advances, the practice of formative assessment is examined in Chapter 3. The purpose of this chapter is to consider the ways in which formative assessment helps to promote learning. The way in which formative assessment has been defined and altered through its use within the national framework is examined. This gives rise to a shift in the use and a clear need for teachers to continue with formative assessment at a classroom level which is not accounted for in national require-ments. The process of formative assessment (not defined by national demands) is explored in terms of concepts of research. From the perspective of qualitative analysis the task of formative assessment requires interpretation, judgement and a recognition of intuition as a key component of practice. Without such acknowledgement formative assessment is unlikely to serve its purpose of helping to advance learning.

Together, Chapters 2 and 3 provide the background of theory in both assessment and learning which are fundamental to subsequent considerations. The focus in Chapter 4 shifts to a more applied context. It examines the way in which assessment in Year 6 impacts on teaching and learning. The chapter is based on the insights gained from a small-scale study in which eleven Year 6 teachers and their pupils share their experiences and views. The study is set into the context of end of Key Stage 2 testing by exploring the types of knowledge and understanding assessed and the skills required to demonstrate these in the tests. The ways in which teachers structure the Year 6 experience so that the curriculum is 'suspended' and revision promoted is explored. The realities of the Year 6 experience are examined in relation to some of the theoretical insights outlined in Chapters 2 and 3. It is argued that the core strategies which are considered essential for effective test revision should be seen as central to teaching and learning and not as an inconvenience and diversion from learning. In this context, the revision for testing is seen as an important aspect of learning. The relationship between learning and assessment illustrates that preparation for assessment can be a positive aspect of learning.

The relationship between learning and assessment is further developed in Chapters 5 and 6. The focus in both these chapters is on pupil self-assessment. In Chapter 5 the emphasis is on a school-based initiative which gives the opportunity to examine self-assessment in action. Although the initiative is not offered as a model for more general use, it is detailed so that insights can be teased out from it. These are developed in Chapter 6 together with a more developed theoretical rationale for self-assessment. The chapter outlines key assumptions, principles and practices for self-assessment which recognise the development of metacognition within a framework of self-regulation. The argument developed here leads to the conclusion in Chapter 7.

In conclusion, the synthesis of the arguments developed advocate that any conceptualisation of assessment must recognise that, if it is to impact on learning, it must form part of learning. Thus, the notion of assessment as learning is advanced. Additionally, the chapter locates the realities of this position in a framework of teacher professionalism. It recognises that any new conceptual-isations or initiatives have to be seen to fit in to the 'modernised' teaching profession and be seen as attainable and desirable by teachers. The commitment of teachers and their continued concern for pupil learning are essential if the education of our children is to develop in the way that it might. We may light some fires, but what education must address more specifically is how do we keep them burning?

Chapter 2

Pupil learning and assessment

Introduction

When interviewing prospective students for primary teacher training, candidates are often asked: 'If you had to identify the most important thing a child learns whilst at primary school, what would it be?' This question usually invokes puzzlement as well as momentary panic in some cases. Although a record has not been kept of responses, all candidates, without exception over the last three years have responded in similar ways. They have identified issues concerning attitudes towards learning, ability to communicate or relationships to others. Some candidates pre-empted their response by indicating the importance of identifying specific skills such as reading or numeracy. Often they continued to outline more general skills and attitudes. The reasons for this may be varied. Interviewees may choose to avoid specific answers. They may well realise the dangers involved in nailing their colours to the mast. Of course, candidates may be unaware of the principal precise aims of primary education. Their failure to identify such aims may require significant attitudinal changes as they seek to survive in the current climate of primary education. On completion of a year's Post Graduate Certificate in Education (PGCE) training under the regime of circular 4/98 (DfEE 1988a: 181), their answer to this question may be very different!

Such a scenario projects a dimension of a much larger issue in primary education. This relates to individual teachers' perceptions of their priorities for learning to those they teach in the classroom. The extent to which teachers have a view of pupil learning which may not be completely consistent with the demands of the National Curriculum programmes of study or the numeracy and literacy strategies has not been closely researched. Bennett *et al.* (1984)

highlight the difficulties which they believed teachers had in relating teaching, learning and the curriculum conceptually. On the basis of his exploration of a large number of theories, mainly of a psychological nature, relating pupil learning to teaching and curriculum issues Bennett offers an explanation of the ambivalence sensed by teachers in their quest to identify these theories which effectively inform their practice. He advances the notion that theories take limited account of the complexities of classroom life. The potential value of such theories seems, therefore, to be marginalised by teachers.

In citing Doyle's work, Bennett (1984: 5) indicates that classroom environments are complex places in which teachers and pupils adapt to each other and where the created environment impacts on them both. Doyle's model of classroom learning processes proceeds on the assumption that 'learning is a covert, intellectual activity which proceeds in the socially complex, potentially rich environment'. If this perspective relates to teachers' experiences in carrying out their role then there are clear restrictions to the applications of many theories of learning to teaching contexts.

Identifying the prominency of complexity by no means excuses careful exploration of the issues. It is recognised that one of the aims of schooling is to promote pupil learning – yet we are not all agreed about what should be prioritised to comprise such learning. Furthermore, there remains considerable disagreement as to how learning occurs. It might be said that since the adoption of the National Curriculum we are nearer to agreeing what should be learnt. However, the ways in which learning occurs seems to be rather sidetracked from what are identified as more pressing mechanisms for teaching curriculum content with the main aim of measuring and raising standards.

It must be recognised that the current lack of attention given to processes of learning are not solely the result of the National Curriculum and accompanying assessments. They may, however, legitimise its demise. As the 1970s drew to a close with the change of government following the 'winter of discontent' (1979), the era of progressivism began to be overshadowed by the emergence of the 'new right'. Debate which had often been focused on teaching methods (e.g. Galton et al. 1980, Bennett 1976) was shifting towards curriculum entitlement. Central to research and discussion on teaching style and methods seemed to be issues related to processes of pupils' learning. Even though opinions were diverse (for example the many and varied responses to Bennett's work) learning seemed central to discussion. With the shifting emphasis to curriculum entitlement during the 1980s and 1990s, it is the product of learning and its measurement through assessment which seems now to have taken prominence. Some of the reasons for this are discussed elsewhere.

The combination of teachers finding that many theories of learning take inadequate account of classroom realities – together with the National Curriculum omitting to consider learning processes – provides a context for this chapter. Although processes of pupils' learning are largely inarticulated there are implicit theories of learning which are evident relating to National Curriculum, assessment and teaching requirements. This chapter tries to highlight the ways in which pupil learning is conceptualised through both National Curriculum and assessment frameworks. Additionally, it seeks to relate these notions to more constructive theories of pupil learning which will form a foundation for the way in which subsequent chapters seek to outline strategies for enhancing learning through assessment.

Making the implicit explicit in identifying theories of learning in the National Curriculum and assessment framework

Any attempt to tease out assumptions about the processes of pupil learning could be construed as inappropriate. To outline the parameters and essence of a perspective, when it is inferred and not articulated or even recognised by its authors, may be tantamount to unjustly imposing interpretations which were never intended. However, the notion that pupils' learning is to be influenced and indeed improved seems to provide one of the main purposes of the introduction of the National Curriculum (NC). The language used to portray the intended impact of the NC is crucial for grasping underlying theory. The consultation document, which set out the National Curriculum framework in 1987, stated:

> we must raise standards consistently, and at least as quickly as they are rising in competitor countries.
>
> (para 6)

> A national curriculum backed by clear assessment arrangements will help to raise standards of attainment . . .
>
> (para 8)

It is assumed that raising standards has a link with improving pupil learning. However, as Davis (1998: 7) points out, improvement in specific performance targets may not relate to an increase in 'real' learning. It seems that one of the main interpretations required relates to distinctions between achievement, performance and learning. The NC consultation document refers to learning just eight times (*learning* {five times – paras. 16, 18, 26, 36ii, 82} *learn* {one – para. 8iii} *learnt* {two – paras. 9ii, 28}). However the terms, performance and achievement, linked to raising standards, feature frequently and prominently throughout.

The language here, together with the curriculum recommendations which became the NC, seem to offer a very specific model of learning. By prescribing the subject domains, knowledge content and targets to be assessed the National Curriculum conforms to an objectives model. Claims that the whole package was 'revolutionary' (Thatcher in a pre-election interview with Sir Donald English, quoted in Simon 1988: 11) on the one hand, yet on the other, offered a 'proven and essential way towards raising standards' (NC 1987: para. 23) suggested an interesting paradox. The level of national prescription, the methods of consultation, the structure of policy implementation may well have been revolutionary but the model being promoted certainly was not. The rise of Taylorism within industry in the early twentieth century provided a model linking behaviour and performance which has had a strong influence in education. By carefully regulating input, identified outcomes could be created in the most effective way. Ralph Tyler made more specific applications to education in 1949. The fundamental idea required curriculum objectives to be prespecified and measured in terms of student behaviour. The processes involved in translating curriculum objectives into changed behaviour were not considered problematic. A 'scientific' approach to teaching and learning, which had demonstrated its worth in both industrial and military contexts was thus advanced.

Complementing the objectives model was the development of behaviourism within psychology. A key proponent, Skinner (1968), applied his principles of behaviour modification to teaching. He described the teacher's role mechanically in the task of 'arranging the contingencies of reinforcement' which would result in changes in pupil behaviour. Skinner's theory of learning (1969) requires that pupils experienced a stimulus. This would yield a response or behaviour by the pupil. The teacher must reinforce the behaviour positively, if the behaviour corresponds with the desired outcome, or negatively if the teacher wants to minimise the chances of that behaviour being repeated. Under this theory, it is assumed that if the curriculum is structured properly and teachers offer the appropriate reinforcement, learning will proceed, irrespective of the motivation, interests or other personal considerations of pupils. Behaviourism assumes that an individual is essentially passive (or perhaps reactive) in a determining environment. The substance of learning is presumed to exist independently of a learner. By controlling the stimulus learning can be shaped and modified to predetermined intentions.

Both the behaviourist model and the objectives model have been subject to sustained attack over nearly three decades (e.g. Lawton 1983; Bruner 1961, 1966). The decision to ground the framework of the National Curriculum into a model which draws extensively from these models seems intriguing. Evidently the government's responses to the issues highlighted by many who have critiqued these perspectives range from regarding their points of concern as irrelevant to the aims and intentions of the recent reforms or being outweighed by other positive benefits. In seeking to tease out the underlying rationale for teaching, learning, assessment and curriculum development within the national framework, a critique of the foundations of these perspectives is offered by examining perspectives and assumptions related to individuals, knowledge and society.

The role of the learner

The individual, in both behaviourism and the objectives model, is regarded as the source of a desired product or effect. The individual is affected by the structure of defined events and contexts. There is little recognition of individually initiated processes, although behaviour that might appear purposive on the part of an individual is explained as being a product of certain stimuli which might have been received in a more powerful way by certain individuals. Contemporary neo-behaviourists, who recognise a more holistic rather than atomistic pathway to learning by describing the effects of combinations of stimuli (stimulus situations) rather than individual stimuli, are still grounded in the assumption that complex learning is controlled by the combination of stimuli given. Similarly within the objectives model, individual differences accorded little attention. All children are expected to demonstrate the objectives identified. They have no scope to shape, negotiate or deviate from these objectives. Together these theories underpin the role of the individual pupil as a mechanical agent who will react to the contexts and information given to him/her. Fundamental opposition to this view of the individual learner is offered later in the chapter in relation to the individual's engagement in the process of learning as well as in relation to the individual's involvement in shaping the product of learning.

Recognising that pupils have a central role in the learning process through their cognitive interactions provides a key challenge for both the objectives model and behaviourism. If learning is regarded as involving an individual, actively in engaging with knowledge and perceptions, the whole process becomes highly complex. From this stance (Gestalt-Field psychology) the individual is recognised as someone who learns by configuring and reconfiguring knowledge so that it relates to existing ideas and learning. The learner is active in interpreting the environment. Although this can lead to highly idiosyncratic perspectives. By recognising that pupils will interpret their learning contexts in ways which vary according to their previous experiences, as well as to their internal cognitive processes, some account can be made for the vast differences in learning displayed within the same learning environment. Furthermore, learning must be intentional. Unless an individual chooses to interact cognitively with the environment learning will not occur. This perspective places considerable emphasis on the role of the pupil in the process of learning. Although objectives and targets may be established and used to frame learning, the outcomes of learning can not be fully predicted. In order to guide, support and facilitate the learning processes teachers will need to use a repertoire of skills and resources so as to offer pupils the scope to develop insights that are relevant to their own construction of meaning.

The product of learning

Identifying learning objectives within subject specific categories, which are to be learnt from comprehensive teaching programmes (programmes of study), presents a framework which is tightly aligned to the objectives model. Underlying this model are several assumptions:

- knowledge can be represented through traditional subjects;
- what is worth knowing can be reduced to objective statements;

- objective statements can be structured to present a sequential, logical, linear progression for learning;
- learning can be accurately measured through rigorous assessments of achievement against the learning objectives.

It seems extraordinary that a curriculum designed to serve the nation in the twenty-first century varies little from the Board of Education's curriculum of 1904. A wealth of developmental work before the National Curriculum sought to break down subject barriers, and resulted in increased value being placed on areas of the curriculum which cross traditional subject boundaries such as personal and social development, health education, politics, sociology, home economics. Some of these areas of inquiry are less traditional in their approaches. They explore value systems and incorporate moral and political judgements which invite critical and reflective thought. Such perspectives do not easily fit into an objectives model. Hence areas of knowledge which can be more easily reduced to objectives form the curriculum as if they 'were a package of fish and chips' (Simon 1988: 118). Plaskow (in *Forum* 1988: 69) believes that 'at stake is one hundred years of adventure beyond the mere basics'. Similarly, Elliott (1988a: 10) states that 'to translate "structures" into "objectives" or "targets" is to distort the nature of knowledge'. The curriculum is presented as fact, prepared and prescribed externally for the pupil to master. It exists externally, resulting from the contrived social decision making which has been constructed by the government. As Young (1998: 27) contends, '"curriculum as fact" presents the curriculum as a thing, hiding the social relations between the teachers, students and curriculum policy makers who have historically and collectively produced it'. Knowledge thus needs to be transmitted. The extent to which it has been received must be judged by someone other than the learner. It is done in ways which indicate whether a child has understood or misunderstood a concept. There is little scope for ambiguity. In a national attempt to both identify and raise 'standards' Elliott (1989: 32) warns that the focus in the National Curriculum will be on surface knowledge rather than on real understanding. It will

> thereby run the risk of distorting the educational process of developing pupils' powers of understanding in a manner which disconnects the acquisition of knowledge from reflection about the values which should be realised in everyday life.

Related to this perspective Edwards and Mercer (1987) present the view that only 'ritual' knowledge can develop if knowledge is presented in terms of scientific rationality and objective truths. Knowledge would be confined to specific individual experiences and practical procedures.

Taking an opposing view, using Young's analysis, 'curriculum as practice' is promoted. The starting point here is not the structure of knowledge but the way that individuals construct their own knowledge. Concepts, claimed Stenhouse (in Elliott 1998: 28) 'are not so much objects of mastery as a focus for speculation'. The curriculum is regarded as integral to the activities pupils undertake as well as to the ways pupils interact with them. Knowledge is therefore constructed through the collaborative work of teachers and pupils. In Edwards and Mercer's terms it is 'principled', promoting a pragmatic approach to communicating knowledge through discourse.

The very notion of raising standards need not be identified in terms of achievement objectives. What might be identified through the assessment of national objectives will represent a limited dimension of knowledge. Elliott (1988b: 11) suggests that the aim of education and indeed any reforms should be to promote excellence. This, he claims, 'is a process which challenges, engages and stretches people's human powers at the deepest level of their being'. Elliott suggests that excellence is unlikely to conform to predictable outcomes: but it is likely to transcend prescription and be demonstrated by an individual who thinks and engages with knowledge in ways that are imaginative and creative. Thus the National Curriculum, which divorces 'standards' from 'human excellence' and confuses raising standards with a process of standardisation is unlikely to promote excellence (Elliott 1988a).

Eisner (1969: 21), long before the National Curriculum, recognised the limitations of what he called instructional objectives. He identified the need for 'expressive objectives'.

> An expressive objective describes an educational encounter. It identifies a situation in which children are to work, a problem with which they are to cope, a task in which they are to engage; but it does not specify what from that encounter, situation, problem or task, they are to learn. An expressive objective provides both the teacher and the student with an invitation to explore, defer, or focus on issues that are of peculiar interest or

important to the enquirer. An expressive objective is evocative rather than prescriptive.

A tight assessment framework within which the National Curriculum operates provides what increasingly seems to be the main source of identifying learning which will indicate rising standards. It legitimises aspects of learning that drive and shape future curriculum priorities (see Chapter 4). The audience for all these endeavours seems to be beyond the classroom which is now considered.

Learning in society

As already indicated, the National Curriculum assumes that pupils are individual learners. Children are assumed to make progress in relation to the prescribed objectives by learning as isolated individuals. They must demonstrate their knowledge individually through test performance. When viewed as part of a larger system, individuals' achievements are combined to portray the achievements of a school, an LEA or even the nation. It seems evident that the role of the individual is very much intended as a part of a collective form of accountability. There is little intention to promote collaborative learning and identity between and among children. The assumptions and priorities which seem evident here drive through an agenda that accords with both the objectives model and with behaviourism.

The ways in which recent reforms have promoted a particular relationship between pupils and society are briefly outlined. They offer an important context for considering the purpose of reforms and aims in education. The NC consultation document (1987) stated that the NC aimed to:

> equip pupils 'for the responsibilities of citizenship and for the challenges of employment in tomorrow's world'
>
> (para. 4)
>
> offer 'progression, continuity and coherence between its different stages'
>
> (para. 5)
>
> 'raise standards consistently, and at least as quickly as they are rising in competitor countries'
>
> (para. 6)

'equip them (pupils) with the knowledge, skills and understanding that they need for adult life and employment'

(para. 7)

'raise standards by giving a broad, balanced curriculum, setting
clear objectives, providing equal access to the curriculum and
checking progress'

(para. 8)

'allow children to experience curriculum progression even if they
move from one part of the country to another'

(para. 9i)

'enable schools to be more accountable for the education they
offer to their pupils, individually and collectively'

(para. 9ii)

A recurring priority in these aims is for schools to be more
accountable, for Britain to be more competitive and for children to
be better equipped for the employment market in adulthood. Ideas
of progression and continuity also feature. However, they relate to
fulfilling an external prescribed order of progression which may not
match the learning priorities and processes of an individual learner.
The emphasis is on raising standards in order for greater success in
the world economy. The document indicates that there is a crisis
and that there is a tried and tested way to address this crisis through
the National Curriculum. As Quicke (in Moon 1989) asserts the
language of crisis features prominently in persuading us that reform
is not only necessary but possible.

The mechanism for elevating Britain's position in the world
economy was not solely dependent on the National Curriculum. The
Education Reform Act (1988) which put the NC on to the statutes
had a more significant impact. As Barber (1996: 49) asserts the act
'set out to create a market within the school system'. The intentions
here are more complex. For a market model to exist there must clearly
be a product and a group of interested consumers. Recognition of
parental interest and involvement in education was evident in Better
Schools (1985) and continued in the NC legislation. Parents were, in
principle, given greater freedom and choice in deciding appropriate
schooling for their children. In order for the market mechanism to
operate there must be differences which are conveyed in accessible

forms. The issue for consideration is how the National Curriculum, aimed at providing uniformity and consistency, will ensure that choice and difference exist in the education marketplace. At face value, as Tomlinson (1989: 52) states, 'a national curriculum and a market in education cannot be compatible in any logic we understand'. With the curriculum becoming regulated and, more recently, teaching being directed (through literacy and numeracy strategies) on what basis will parents make their judgements? League tables of pupils' test results together with Ofsted reports for each school provide evidence and information for parents in the marketplace. The insights which these forms of information may offer, as well as the extent to which parents can actually exercise choice in the marketplace are, however, contentious.

Of importance in this discussion is the way in which learning is both shaped and interpreted within society. Through the market mechanism pupil learning is presented in collective forms in order to indicate the success of a school in relation to a competitor school. It is the basis upon which school is set against school within league tables. Levels of learning, as measured through Standard Assessment Tests (SATs), are now the indicators of the success of primary schools in society. From the aims set out in the National Curriculum consultation document the standard of achievement gained is intended to contribute to a more successful economy in which pupils are better equipped for employment. The distinction here between a society and an economy is muddled. During the Thatcher years it was clear that the economy was the overarching concern – even within education. Indeed, Thatcher stated that there is no such thing as society. The continuation of the National Curriculum and the drive for standards under New Labour have also been accompanied by a view that individuals have a particular role within society. Hence the introduction of guidelines for personal, social and health education and citizenship in Curriculum 2000 offer an additional direction. Their currency within the curriculum, since the law does not back them, is not yet discernible.

Whether the National Curriculum and its accompanying assessments are designed to promote the economy, society or both, there seems to be a fundamental omission. There appears to be no formal regard for the role of the National Curriculum in helping children to be better equipped for childhood. The emphasis is on equipping them for the 'challenges of employment in tomorrow's world' (NC 1987: para. 4). The extent to which pupils' learning might be linked to their current, existing and short-term needs and priorities is given little recognition.

For education to feature so prominently as a mechanism for achieving goals for society and the economy is unprecedented in this country. Details of learning seemed to be construed in a way in which only expected outcomes are valued. The process of pupil learning has been marginalised from policy discussion. The term 'learning' seems almost to be taking on a new meaning. This, as this chapter explores, is implicit in policy initiatives and reform priorities. There is, however, a new perspective on learning which merits brief consideration in relation to the current discussion – the 'learning society'.

Young (1998: 141) suggests that the notion of a learning society is an example of a 'utopia becoming an ideology'. Barber (1996) on the other hand, presents his vision for re-engineering in education. Its aim accords with the purpose for reform laid out in the National Curriculum (DES 1988c). Thus to increase success in competition with the countries of the Pacific Rim calls for us to 'reinvent the learning process' (Barber 1996: 249). Creating a *learning society* is promoted as the ambitious aim for our education policy. Barber contends that it will allow everyone to both

> benefit from and to contribute to the flows of knowledge and information on which our future depends. In other words, a learning society is one in which every person is an active learner. Britain would cease to be a nation of shopkeepers and becomes instead a nation of learners.
>
> (Barber 1996: 241)

Achieving such a goal will not be accomplished through steps to school improvement. Making schools more responsible and accountable, as has been the case in recent years, ultimately will have limited impact. The reason, Barber claims, is because it 'fails to address sufficiently the overall inadequacy of British cultural attitudes to education and learning' (p. 248). The solution, he asserts, is to seek the learning potential for each individual and to recognise that learning is not confined to schools. The process of learning, which has been neglected, must be prioritised along with the product of learning. If standards are to rise and the education of this country is to be transformed the assumptions and rules which have permeated our education system over recent years must be overturned rather than tinkered with. The shift in emphasis, therefore, would be from 'institutions to individuals and from teachers to learners' (p. 253). The vision begins with the individual learner and his or her learning needs.

The recognition that schools are not solely responsible for the standards of education in this country and that the individual needs of pupils are central to effective learning feature prominently in this book. The mechanisms and rationale which Barber offers, however, are more cautiously regarded. The model of re-engineering presented is grounded in notions of management and enterprise which are high risk. Some fail, some succeed. The casualties along the way are part of the development process. Being radical and revolutionary offers no guarantees. Although it is recognised that the failures of tradition provide only a platform for progress, the casualties of revolution may rock education to its core. The 'Learning Game' which Barber describes, as yet, has no rules. Whoever plays the game, there will be both winners and losers. Despite elevating the status of pupils' learning, the processes of learning are not outlined. Only the range and contexts of learning opportunities are offered. Trying to advance a resolution on such a basis seems premature, however commendable.

Young, in exploring the perspectives of a learning society offers his own model – the connective model. What is advanced here differs significantly from Barber's individual learning promises. Young (1998: 50) advocates 'learning relationships'. This, he claims, requires the type of learning to be examined. Credentialism (gaining qualifications) or gaining access to greater learning opportunities is insufficient alone. The remainder of this chapter seeks to outline how learning might take place. It attempts to present a learning framework which is compatible with the processes of recognising, raising and measuring standards, yet has the learner at the heart of the process. It is from this basis that the role of assessment as part of the learning process can be constructed in the following chapters.

Learning – an alternative perspective

The purpose of this section is to explore foundations and priorities for learning. These attempt to be both ideologically and pragmatically grounded. Ideologically, they lean to constructivism, yet they seek to recognise the national context of the curriculum and assessment. The ideology of learning implicit in national developments is identified as contrary to that which is promoted here. There is no question of mixing ideologies since their opposing nature does not allow reconciliation. Nevertheless, compromises must be made in order to function in contexts in which competing values exist. The level of compromise will vary according to individuals' value orientations. Identifying and developing learning theory seeks to encourage the coexistence of a learning agenda with an achievement agenda.

The fundamental premises underlying the perspectives advanced here are:

- the learner is at the centre of the learning process;
- meanings are socially constructed;
- knowledge is context bound (situated).

The centrality of the learner

This first premise might immediately be regarded as child-centred progressivism. Unambiguous interpretation of this statement, however, cannot be assumed. Ideologically, progressivism directly opposes traditionalism, moving the emphasis away from the content of traditional subject based knowledge to the process of learning. The prominence of progressive education was particularly promoted through the Plowden Report (1967). At the start of Chapter 2 of this report it states that 'at the heart of the education process lies the child'. The ideology promoted is best seen from the following extract in Chapter 15 of the report.

> A school is not merely a teaching shop, it must transmit values and attitudes. It is a community in which children learn to live first and foremost as children and not as future adults. In family life children learn to live with people of all ages. The school sets out deliberately to devise the right environment for children, to allow them to be themselves, to develop in the way and at the pace appropriate to them. It tries to equalize opportunities for creative work. It insists that knowledge does not fall into neatly separate compartments and that work and play are not opposite but complementary. A child brought up in such an atmosphere at all stages of his education has some hope of becoming a balanced and mature adult and of being able to live in, to contribute to, and to look critically at the society of which he forms a part.
>
> (Vol. 1, pp. 187–8)

The legacy of the agenda for primary education which was advocated through Plowden endures (Galton *et al.* 1999; Silcock 1999). Its original emergence was to combat the narrow and restricted practices prompted by traditionalist ideologies, yet after years of its supposedly underlying primary practice from the 1970s, it has been cited as one of the reasons for the reintroduction of the back to basics National Curriculum (Silcock 1999).

Considerable research into primary practice has involved an examination of the extent to which progressivism has been prominent in schools. Galton *et al.* (1999), for example, highlight the findings of the ORACLE study which explored primary classrooms during the mid to late 1970s. This study typified group work, children carrying out a range of different tasks and the teacher moving around the classroom interacting with groups of pupils. Very little seemed to have changed when the study was repeated in 1996. The surface appearance of these classrooms seemed to convey progressive principles. However, clear evidence of the centrality of the pupil in the learning process was not convincing. Alexander (1992: 193) indicated that research shows only the 'myth of progressivism'. Children apparently working in groups were in fact working individually on tasks which required no collaboration and were clearly directed by the teacher. On the one hand it was difficult to identify progressivism in practice and be certain what it was, yet Chris Woodhead (1995), HM Chief Inspector of Schools, claimed progressivism, which continued to dominate primary practice, was the greatest barrier to raising standards.

Mixed reception and interpretation of progressivism has contributed to some confusion over what it is and how it might continue in a changing educational climate. Far from subverting the national call for raising standards and promoting accountability, progressivism may enhance it. Silcock (1999) offers both analysis and reconstruction as he presents 'new progressivism'. Here the ideology is reconsidered within contemporary contexts so that some of the errors and assumptions are clarified. In this new progressivism the child remains the centre of the learning process. However, further investigation is required to clarify the meaning of this assertion, and to justify the situation it represents. For the purposes of this chapter, understanding processes of learning which are congruent with national policy requirements is necessary in order to construct the new relationship between learning and assessment which this book advances.

How pupils learn

The notion of constructivism is a prominent feature of much research on learning. This was initially linked to Piaget's ideas of the development of learning. According to Piaget children actively constructed their own understandings of the world around. They are their own development agents, genetically propelled to interact with the environment in ways which progressively shape and restructure their conceptual understanding. Teachers have a role in helping to create learning contexts which help pupils construct understanding at appropriate levels by enabling assumptions to be challenged and consolidated. Piaget offers some insights into the processes by which cognition advances. Through the processes of assimilation, accommodation and equilibrium individuals are able to categorise and recategorise concepts. Given appropriate experiences, these may become complex and interconnected. The processes through which the mind develops are, however, rather vague.

Neuro-scientists have grappled with the issues of the development of the mind for many years. The neural basis of memory and learning has been explored in an attempt to identify whether or not learning and memory functions inhabit discrete or mosaic locations in the brain and how neurological changes result in learning. The brain makes order out of all the information which bombards it. In order to do this there must be some process of selection and self-organisation. Through his studies on the immune system, Edelman (1987) sought to explain how the body functions selectively. When a foreign body enters the body the immune system selects one of a vast number of antibodies to attack the invader, multiply and so destroy the disease throughout the body. The mechanism he identified, for which he shared the Nobel prize in 1972, he called the 'clonal selection'. Edelman extended his theory to the study of the nervous system in order to ascertain whether a similar sort of selection process occurred when new information or experiences are encountered, and the brain seeks to accommodate them. He thought that groups of cells would compete to deal with the new situations. So when a child experiences the world around it is not a frenzied chaotic place in which no sense can be made. Fundamental selections are made based on innate predispositions arising from early neurone development as well as from the perception of values and feelings already categorised. As an individual deals with new experiences groups of neurones are selectively strengthened and new connections are made. The brain is active in this process. However, the links between the neurological connections in the brain, the experiences which help to shape them and the developing behaviour and learning of the child requires more advanced thinking. In order for neurone connection to be more complex, and allow more sophisticated thinking, groups of neurones must be interconnected making complex concept maps. Thus to perceive and comprehend the world around, an individual neurone must select groups of neurones which are then strengthened and interconnected forming 'maps'. Successful linkage of these groupings is reinforced by the individual as s/he feel that they have interpreted reality (their reality). Continual communication between maps which Edelman calls 'reentrant signalling' allows the individual to perceive complex constructs, and to revisit them. Higher order consciousness and thinking occurs through re-entrant signalling through two steps – the linking of memory with current perception and, secondly, the linking of symbolic memory with conceptual centres formed in the brain. Through these processes an individual may become conscious of consciousness and thus achieve higher order thinking skills which separates them from other living things. Therefore the learning and understanding which children have of the world around is not a simple matter of many single images but a perpetually balanced and fluctuating view made of interpreted interconnected maps and many recategorisations. For each individual the complex interconnections will be different. Thus an individual comes to know his/her world uniquely. Edelman's theory provides one of the only explanations for the development of mind in contemporary psychology and neurology. Furthermore, it complements constructivist theory in the way that an individual comes to know the world. It sits easily with Piaget's theory offering more in-depth explanations of the mechanisms which Piaget recognises in form but not in their formation.

The view of constructivism which Piaget's theory conveys is seen as limited in that Piaget recognises the learner as an isolated individual interacting independently with the environment. The influence of context, of other individuals, of language, of intention are all regarded as unimportant. Those who have criticised Piaget (and there are many – e.g. Donaldson 1978) have highlighted the role of language and social interaction as being important in the process of learning. Vygotsky (1962) emphasised the role of language in the generation of thought. Language, he claimed, was a key tool for the development of cognition. It is, however, ostensibly social, thus recognising that learning has a social dimension.

Learning as social construction

Vygotsky's theory requires more than just incorporating a social dimension into Piaget's theory as some neo-Piagetian thinkers have attempted (Valsiner 1992; Nelson *et al.* 1998). Vygotsky's theory requires a fundamentally different understanding of the role of purposes of 'others' in the learning process. The learner cannot be regarded in isolation from others. In school, both teacher and peers have a part to play in the learning process. The process through which social interaction influences the learning processes can be compared to an apprenticeship model of learning. The novice works alongside an expert in the zone of proximal development. With the help and guidance of the teacher, the pupil is able to achieve a higher level of achievement than s/he could achieve alone. For Vygotsky the premise for learning is social interaction. For Piaget, on the other hand, his belief that young children are unable to take on the perspectives and thinking of others, because of egocentrism, renders social construction virtually impossible rather than undesirable at an early age. Piaget does, however, recognise the role which peers (as equals) may have in the learning process. A child may well take issue with another child's thinking and through arguing come to reconsider his/her perspective. Both children must have a common language and system of ideas as they come to adjust their opinions. Their thinking is logical and encourages cognitive conflict which Piaget identifies as essential for learning. The role of 'others' in the learning processes is thus very different from those suggested by Vygotsky. Rogoff (1999) suggests that the form of learning being undertaken may affect the processes of pupil learning. Thus, formal logical mathematical learning may fit into Piaget's model of learning more easily than the learning of skills and more culturally related knowledge. Such a view suggests that the formation of knowledge has different legitimising processes and contexts. This would clearly be an oversimplistic explanation within the primary school curriculum. Such a distinction is thus not considered helpful. Silcock helps to explain the reasons for this. As a learner, a pupil must accept his/her role as novice and be willing to engage in social learning interactions. S/he must become a 'co-constructor' of knowledge (Silcock 1999). Even operations of mind which might be classified as logico-mathematical are situated in cultural, historical and institutional settings – they are in Wertsch's terms (1991) 'socio-cultural'.

Pupils are recognised as novices working alongside those who are experienced. They participate in communities which seek to develop and extend their conceptual participation. Additionally, they seek to develop their practice culturally and socially. Lave and Wenger (1999) characterise the pupils' role as 'legitimate peripheral participation'. This accepts that the pupil is in the role of learner but that s/he has a particular status within the community. Any changes in knowledge are subsumed by changes in identity. The community of learning has a particular context. Thus, the whole context of learning features in the learning process. This makes it difficult to be sure that any specific knowledge components which may be identified to be taught in abstract or general ways will be learnt in the ways which might be expected. It is contended (for example by Wertsch 1991; Lave and Wenger 1999; Rogoff 1999) that all learning is 'situated'. The teacher, within this context is 'a human event, not a transmission device' (Bruner 1986: 126) and pupils' learning will always be embedded in context. This has implications for the way which we identify learning. Our current modes of measuring and identifying learning through assessment and testing assume that knowledge can be transferred from the classroom context to the test paper unproblematically. Accepting such a simplistic notion of learning transfer is incompatible with the view of learning outlined here.

It may be, as Davis (1998) suggests, that some knowledge and action is less situated than other types of knowledge. So, throwing and catching a ball, he claims, is likely to be learnt with less impact of context than more complex skills and knowledge. Nevertheless, context is evident in all knowledge. If there is an expectation that knowledge might be transferred from one situation to another the fundamental assumption advocated here is that cognitive transfer is social rather than abstract. What is meant by this is that 'the potential transfer between situations is shaped by the social practices in which the people learn the activities' (Greeno et al. 1993: 102). In order to learn in new contexts and to demonstrate learning, the context and framing of the knowledge must be personally interpreted within a particular (particular to the child) social culture and context. In the classroom teachers can help pupils make connections between different learning contexts, and use knowledge in settings which they can coconstruct. In Rogoff's (1999) terms this allows the 'expert' to play a supportive role in helping the 'novice' bridge the gap between old and new knowledge within shared contexts.

The issues and theories here are to some extent developmental. The precise mechanisms at work are not exactly defined, and may continue to defy some definition. Nonetheless an attempt to prioritise competing tensions is vital. As Pollard (1999: 58) asserts: 'The socio-cultural model is impressive in its depth and vision . . . Research is still at a creative and formative point with many leads and directions being followed.'

Conclusion

The ground covered in this chapter outlines perspectives of learning embedded in the national framework. The objectives model and behaviourism describe the views of learning which would seem to support existing curriculum and assessment policies. The function of learning is identified as being located in the market and economic contexts of competition and improvement. Only prespecified areas of the curriculum seem to hold currency in the public arena. Any notion that individual pupil learning cannot be easily disassembled from learning contexts is ignored. This framework advances by increasing the pressure on teachers to lever up standards through more rigorous teaching and assessment. Policing of the system through inspection and benchmarking serves to ensure that the pressure on teachers is sustained. An alternative explanation of pupil learning is offered through developing socio-cultural learning theory. Any progress in knowledge is located within a learning context and is achieved through the coconstruction of knowledge. Recognising learning thus requires far more complex understanding of individuals, relationships and contexts. Within the classroom the teacher must mediate between national requirements and individual needs. The processes of mediation which have already been identified in post-national curriculum research (Dann and Simco 2000) offers an optimistic view of teachers' skills in reconciling the tensions which could so easily dominate classroom practice. These, together with the reconsideration of teachers' professional development (see Chapter 7) forms a vital context for the developing argument in this book.

Chapter 3

Formative assessment

Introduction

Formative assessment has been more prominently promoted following the post-1987 educational reforms. Ironically, it seemed that its potential role and function had been highlighted and formalised because of fears associated with the emergence of a national summative assessment framework. At a simplistic level, formative assessment should inform the teaching and learning process. It thus seems to imply immediacy as well as detail. This chapter seeks to identify the role and status of formative assessment within a developing national context. Additionally, it explores some fundamental issues related to its foundations and form which link it to common models of research, and considers the role of the teacher in terms of the importance of judgement and intuition.

Coined by Scriven (1967), the term 'formative evaluation' focuses on the processes and mechanisms for improving the curriculum. Its subsequent application to student learning was linked to summative evaluation tests. Formative evaluation was welcomed as a tool for helping the student, teacher and curriculum constructor to 'improve what they wish to do' (Bloom *et al.* 1971: 117). Unfortunately, however, emphasis on 'improvement' within formative assessment often left unexplored the meaning of improvement. What seems to be evident is that the function of assessment, in contributing to positive change and improvement, is emphasised over the processes involved.

Tunstall and Gipps (1996: 389) explain formative assessment as

teachers using their judgements of children's knowledge or understanding to feedback into the teaching process and to determine for individual children whether to re-explain the task/concept, to give further practice on it, or move on to the next stage.

On this view the processing of information is the main, if not the sole, responsibility of teachers in formative assessment. Such responsibility is hardly consistent with constructivist theories of learning which facilitate the prospect of assessment promoting learning. More than that, though, the concept of feedback requires a more serious and problematical treatment, as suggested in Chapter 6. Similarly, the TGAT report (1998a: para. 27) emphasised the need for appropriate 'information' to be collected which would help diagnose strengths and weaknesses. As Torrance and Pryor (1998) suggest, these views seem more related to evaluation than assessment.

Formative assessment within the national curriculum framework

Interpretations of formative assessment in the late 1980s and 1990s seemed to be made within the rapidly emerging and developing national context. They were a product of their time. The TGAT (1998a) report promoted the national assessment system which would have pupil learning at its heart (para. 3). Furthermore, the system should be formative in that the results should provide a basis for decisions about pupils' further learning needs (para. 5). The assessments, to be based on criterion referenced criteria, would be judged both by teachers through teacher assessment and through externally provided methods and procedures. The supplementary report (1988b) stated that 'neither should reign supreme' (para. 11). Although acknowledging that no country has yet devised a system which has well-developed links between formative purposes and progression, the proposals which were presented boasted of being 'evolutionary and radical' (para. 19). There was no evidence promoted for the presumed success that the system claimed it would bring. Notions of learning underpinning assessment, as well as the way in which the proposed system would supposedly ensure progression and coherence, were not explored or examined. The use of the term 'formative assessment' had two meanings in the report. First, it is linked to pupil learning and its development. Here, it is closely aligned with diagnostic assessment which might be needed to diagnose more specific strengths and weaknesses. Second, the use of the term 'formative' in the 'summary and conclusion' section of the report provided an additional perspective, which seemed to move the term into an evaluative frame – 'the system is also required to be formative at the national level, to play an active part in raising standards of attainment' (para. 222). The claim that formative assessment should raise national standards implied that the level of detail of assessment was not so much related to individual pupils' learning but to aggregated pupil data indicating national trends. The level of detail required, and thus the type of learning which might advance at a national level from such 'formative' purposes, seemed to add another layer of potential ambiguity. As the proposal for a national system progressed to implementation, the balance between formative and diagnostic purposes with summative and evaluative purposes, were presented in a way which would offer unity and manageability. Such manageability did not seem apparent in schools and among teachers. The different emphases in assessment purposes seemed to operate more and more in tension.

The proposal for the four assessment purposes (formative, summative, diagnostic and evaluative) to be served simultaneously was outlined with an emphasis on formative assessment. In order to fulfil summative and evaluative purposes it was suggested that an aggregation of data gleaned from formative means would be the foundation for all assessments (para. 25). Warnings were given about attempting to tackle the formative emphasis of the stated assessment purpose by collecting data from summative or evaluative processes (paras. 25, 221)

The model presented within TGAT laid the foundations for a particular orientation on formative assessment. The link between a process of assessment, identifying learning needs, with imposed assessment criteria in the National Curriculum, determined the focus of formative assessment. In this national context formative assessment was presented as unchallenged. Professional consensus, which accepted and tried to work with the TGAT model as good practice, became apparent.

Foundations for TGAT

Essentially the nature of formative assessment proposed by TGAT can be related to part of the behaviourist tradition which seeks to identify mastery against a range of stated objectives. The particular orientation of the assessment framework can be closely linked to the work in the field of graded assessment/testing (e.g. Pennycuick 1988). The central concern within graded assessment was to overcome some of the main drawbacks of the public examination system. It aimed to offer the following:

- assessment designed to determine whether or not mastery has been attained;
- entry of pupils for the tests or assessments when they are likely to succeed;
- pupils' mastery at one level before proceeding to the next.

(Adapted from Pennycuick 1988: 70)

These principles seemed to reflect the fundamental basis of the TGAT proposals in terms of mastery, readiness and progression. They have an obvious and particular link to learning theory through behaviourism and linear learning hierarchies, yet these links are not discussed, explained or clarified in the report.

The nature of formative assessment advocated was multi-dimensional. In particular, the emerging emphasis concerned the 'build up a comprehensive picture of the overall achievements of a pupil . . .' (para. 25). To this end, it was suggested that 'a broad range of assessment instruments sampling a broad range of attainments targets', should be used (para. 58). Such an approach was advocated and supported in a range of writing on assessment. HMI (1991: 13) stated that 'good assessment practice involved a carefully balanced combination of observation, questioning, discussion and marking'. The report from the Schools Examination and Assessment Council (SEAC 1990) concerning the development and use of records of achievement in primary schools emphasised the need for a broad range of assessment evidence to be valued and shared. Additionally, the controversial report from Alexander *et al.* (1992: 39) stated (seemingly uncontroversially) that 'teachers should . . . create the time and opportunity for assessment and diagnosis to take place, using both observation and interaction . . . (as well as) combine assessment of work completed with assessment of work in progress . . .'. In an attempt to further promote this view as good practice Ofsted's (1993) case study examples of the well-managed classroom summarised good practice in assessment as being 'intuitive and informal, based on discussion and observation', but this is supplemented by note taking and the recording of observations and other attainment evidence such as test results (p. 31). Gradually, the view that formative assessment was the way forward gained considerable status. Amidst a number of changes in the national context the challenges and demands of the process of formative assessment, portrayed in TGAT and subsequent documents, were taken seriously by teachers.

Transition to teacher assessment

With the development of the National Curriculum subject requirements, primary school teachers were faced with the task of assessing all pupils in relation to the attainment targets in all nine subjects. The fairly soft touch approach of the standard tasks at KS 1 in the pilot tests in 1990 and the full-scale implementation in 1991 required many of the attainment targets to be judged by teachers. Very rapidly the formative nature of assessment, upon which the framework was promoted, was given little acknowledgement. Rather, the process of teacher assessment of the attainment targets became the focus. Initially the link between teachers carrying out the assessment and formative assessment seemed strong. However, throughout much of the 1990s attention was directed away from formative assessment towards a growing pressure on teachers to be more rigorous in their assessment of attainment targets. The emphasis, increasingly, was on teacher assessment and on seeking to ensure that teachers developed the necessary skills to participate in their assessment responsibilities competently and consistently. The number of attainment targets requiring teachers to offer an assessment level was vast. Even following the Dearing review, the expectation that all subjects were assessed and that evidence was carefully considered for all pupils, provided a considerable pressure. Teachers, however, despite this pressure were pleased that their role as assessors seemed to be valued and many sought to fulfil the requirements. The process of transition to the role of teacher assessor was not easy. Pollard *et al.* (1994: 190–1) in the PACE project indicated a number of insights into some of the processes involved. Infant teachers claimed that they assessed frequently for pedagogic reasons and usually did not record these assessments formally. Following the national changes teachers were spending a considerable amount of time on record keeping which formalised much of the work they had previously undertaken. Teachers stated that they lacked confidence in what they were doing in recording, and were reported as having more negative feelings about assessment and record keeping (pp. 196–7). The demands of the SATs transformed assessment from being 'implicit and provisional' to being 'explicit and categoric' (p. 208). These tests required procedures to be more formalised and based on 'explicit collection and labelling of evidence, on explicit acts of assessment and on categoric reporting of children's achievement in terms of a national scale' (p. 208). The structure of the SATs required teachers to assess in a specific way using specified materials. These Key Stage 1 tests relied on teachers' own judgements in interpreting pupils' responses. They helped to provide formal evidence to support other assessment judgements made on a more continual basis.

As SATs developed and were introduced in Key Stages 2 and 3 their nature changed. They were externally marked and involved teacher participation only in terms of test administration. Furthermore, the tests were designed to give an overall subject level in the core subjects. It seemed clear at this stage that teacher assessment was beginning to become marginalised within national testing. Teacher assessments were presented alongside national test results. However, the assertion that 'neither should reign supreme' (para. 11, TGAT supplementary 1988b) was not upheld as the SAT results began to take priority over teachers' judgements, most notably, in any cases of discrepancy.

By the end of the 1990s it was clear that results from the SATs formed the main currency within the educational accountability market. The drive to try to ensure that measurable standards were in the public arena shaped the direction of assessment priorities. As the SATs developed it became increasingly clear that the direction, structure and purpose of testing were far from those envisaged in the TGAT proposals. Alongside these developments guidance was offered to support teachers develop their teacher assessment. SEAC (Schools Examination and Assessment Council), at the end of 1990, offered its 'Guide to Teacher Assessment: Packs A, B and C'. As Daugherty (1995: 70) asserts these 'were long on generalisations and short on down-to-earth practical suggestions on the matters which by then teachers were grappling with'. The notion of teacher assessment as having an important role in national assessment frameworks was not developed through TGAT. Unsurprisingly then, the lack of clarity at this initial stage offered little basis for progression. Attempts to develop practices of teacher assessment in the summative national context often made heavy demands on teachers. Both the function and form of teacher assessment remained unclear. Most teachers were attempting to assess and record individual statements of attainment and also felt that demands for accountability would require them to offer evidence for each judgement (Daugherty 1995: 74–5).

Development of teachers' skills and competence in teacher assessment is extremely variable. With little guidance, it seemed that confidence could not be fully placed in the consistency and reliability of teacher assessments. If the TGAT vision of SATs and teacher assessment, having equal status in the national frameworks, were to be realised, consistency in the approaches to both would be needed.

The great burden which teachers felt they had in conducting their teacher assessments, in a way that was based on rigorous evidence rather than 'only' professional judgement seemed to fuel dissatis-faction (PACE 1994). Teachers were not sure what credibility their judgements were gaining in the public arena of aggregated assess-ments. Without clear clarification and direction it seemed that teacher assessment was being marginalised from policy debate in the primary sector; its existence and continuation being more in the realm of teacher assessment for formative purposes than in the summative national context. The role and status of teacher assessment shifted following the introduction of the National Curriculum. Its original status as an intuitive professional practice, which was interlinked with teaching and learning, shifted (through the TGAT proposals) to being part of both formative and summative assessment frame-works. This has recently moved back towards an emphasis on formative assessment which is not directly linked to national require-ments, albeit with more structure and emphasis on evidence. (Its role and potential is further developed later in this chapter and in subsequent chapters.)

With the assessment agenda being clearly set until 2002 the role of teacher assessment in the national framework is minimal. Interpretation of this reality could be varied: the political and policy direction which culminated in very little emphasis or support being given to teacher assessment could be considered as having been deliberate. Alternatively, it could be that teacher assessment has emerged as receiving less priority with little consistent evidence to promote good practice. Mechanisms devised to develop SATs were experimental and innovative. Yet as revisions and changes emerged the government asserted that STs now offered tried and tested measures. (The term ST – Standard Tests – was introduced in place of SATs). Excellence in schools (1997) states that 'we now have sound, consistent, national measures of pupil achievement for each school at each Key Stage of the National Curriculum'.

There was no determination to establish teacher assessment in a similar vein. The enormity to which the task of teacher assessment grew within the national framework was such that it became virtually an impossible task. Such variety of practice and the varying degrees of confidence attributed to them contributed to the demise of teacher assessment as part of a summative accountability agenda. Thus, the foundation of teacher assessment as formative 'evaluation' was not likely to be perpetuated. Therefore, the role of teacher assessment seemed to be moving towards being school and classroom based.

Developing formative assessment

The process of formative assessment is more related to the ongoing process of teaching and learning than with any national standardised procedure indicated by TGAT. Returning to Tunstall and Gipps' (1996) definition, which prioritised the teachers' role in making a judgement on children's learning that feeds back into the teaching and learning process, the concept is now further explored. Much of the information on formative assessment assumes that the focus of control lies with the teacher. It is s/he who will use assessment information to make decisions about future teaching and learning. As Torrance and Pryor highlight (1998: 12) the pupil 'stands still' between gathering and interpreting assessment information and any ensuing teacher intervention. The pupil seems to be portrayed as passive, learning only as a result of revised or adjusted teacher intervention. In such a scenario, the extent to which formative assessment is a process aimed to help thinking about teaching or is about advancing pupil learning, must be considered. If the latter is to be achieved there must be greater recognition of the pupils' role in understanding, interpreting and internalising the assessment process, as well as the feedback from it. The previous chapter affirmed the primacy of active pupil involvement in learning viewed from a constructivist perspective. Thus, any distinction between teaching, learning and assessment becomes fuzzy with such a complex reciprocity involved. Inherent in the teaching, learning and assessment dynamic are the social relations evident between teacher and pupil as well as between pupils (see Chapter 6). If formative assessment is to relate to the notions of learning previously outlined in Chapter 2 there must be some recognition of the social construction of learning and an individual's interpretation of meaning. In terms of the process of formative assessment, a distinction needs to be drawn between classroom assessment, which identifies how pupils respond to the instruction given so that maximum benefit is achieved, and assessment which probes the teacher/pupil relationship trying to establish limits of learning which pupils can gain with teacher guidance. Newman *et al.* (1989: 77) distinguish between teachers who use assessment to promote change from those who use it to measure change. They recognise both 'assessment by teaching' (dynamic assessment) and 'assessment while teaching'. The latter is seen as an important part of instruction and is often driven by the pressures of classroom life. It seeks to establish the extent of pupil learning in order to modify and direct teaching. 'Assessment by teaching', however, has a fundamentally different basis and is derived from a particular interpretation of Vygotsky's zone of proximal development (ZPD).

> Instead of giving the children a task and measuring how well they do or how badly they fail, one can give the children the task and observe how much and what kind of help they need in order to complete the task successfully.
>
> (Newman *et al.* 1989: 77)

For dynamic assessment to function, a teacher must develop complex sensitivities to the extent, nature and timing of intervention. Giving too much help and support will not allow children to demonstrate the limits of their skills, abilities and knowledge. Teachers need to withdraw their support to leave pupils at the very edge of their abilities. Such skills and judgement requires fine grade assessment strategies. Furthermore, the possible usefulness of this strategy must relate to the extent to which pupils' learning is free to develop without the pressure of predetermined end goals which are within time restraints. In an educational context, which demands a defined pace of learning, this seems rather idealistic. Attempting to incorporate the principles of dynamic assessment, recognising its fundamental assumptions regarding the primacy of controlled intervention to promote learning, need not be impossible. It does, however, require the acceptance of 'inherent ambiguity' (Newman 1989: 88) which allows for and indeed recognises limitations to the use of 'dynamic assessment' within an 'assessment while teaching' framework.

Fundamental to the aims, procedures and outcomes of formative assessment is an understanding of the teachers' role in the process. Newman advocates that the teacher is not so much an assessor/tester but a 'cognitive researcher' qualitatively tracking learning where the route and the end point are not clearly known in advance. The application of a metaphor of 'assessment as research' offers a possible route for exploration which may help to outline and understand processes of formative assessment.

Formative assessment as research

The introduction of a link between assessment and research requires some justification. Of course research, like assessment, has many dimensions, interpretations and assumptions and it may seem over simplistic to parallel the two. Cizek (1997) suggests that assessment might be explored using the metaphor of 'as research design'. He promotes the view that a typical approach to research design would provide a useful starting point for classroom assessment:

> Assessment – like research design – is the purposive configuration of events to acquire information bearing on an important question in a fair, accurate and efficient manner. Conceiving of assessment in this way has the potential to: broaden the universe of valuable educational outcomes that are assessed; reduce redundancy of assessment information; enhance the match between the targets of assessment and the strategies used to gather information about those targets; focus assessments so that they more directly bear on the questions of interest; promote usefulness, meaningfulness, and interpretability of the information yielded by assessments.
>
> (Cizek 1997: 13)

Cizek (1997: 14) promotes five research design procedures, which he applies to the process of assessment. These are represented in the following points:

- Background – consider why assessment is required and what information is needed about pupils. In implementing assessment(s) consider positive and negative factors resulting from the process or processes and who may be affected. Check that the assessment information to be collected is not a duplicate of existing data. If it is intended assessment may well be redundant.
- Purpose – consider the research questions, which the assessment(s) seeks to address. For example, does the assessment seek

to gain information about specific aspects of learning or to identify performance levels? The form in which the assessment information will be collected will influence the extent to which the research questions can be answered and the audience which it can serve.

- Methods – consider a range of strategies and instruments that could be used as the means of gaining the required assessment information. This might include developing new initiatives. The relative merits of time, cost and appropriateness must be weighed up. Additionally, limitations of validity and reliability should be controlled, acknowledged or reduced in accordance with intended audiences and purposes.

- Results – the quality of the assessment data must be examined in order to establish the extent to which it can serve the purposes intended. Additional or supplementary information may need to be added to augment the information collected. Results need to be meaningful to the audiences receiving reports or information. Thus, there may need to be different levels and forms of information presented.

- Discussion – guidance on interpretation is required, which is sensitive to both validity and reliability issues. This will need to be modified and exemplified according to the audience. Key issues may need to be highlighted whilst others offered more tentatively. Questions must be asked about what still remains unanswered or what was not even considered in the designed assessments.

The research design procedure of establishing background information, defining purpose, selecting methods, gathering results/ information and discussing findings is linked to assessment. The research design allows choices to be made at each stage regarding intention and process. It does, however, assume that the purposes of assessment are clear and that results can be elicited and communicated. Within national curriculum assessments the application of this research design to the processes involved seem fairly unproblematic.

As indicated in Chapter 2, certain assumptions prevail regarding the nature of knowledge, individuals and society in teaching, learning and assessment. When looking at research design in assessment contexts a similar set of assumptions must be exposed. First, and of most significance, is the belief in rigour and objectivity. Second, that conclusions are easy to convey. As part of a 'scientific' approach to research a positivist perspective prevails. The assessment method is seen to be neutral, controlling a variety of possible varying elements. Any instrument of assessment used needs to be clearly focused yielding data which is assumed to require minimal interpretation. Consequently, results will be considered objective and context free, available and accessible to a variety of possible audiences. Cumulation of results will allow generalisations to be made which may be used to substantiate, extend or refute theory, policy and/or practice. From this research stance (as with the behaviourist learning tradition) assumptions are made about the way in which individual actions and achievements can be measured. They are considered as context free. Thus, any way in which they may be situated is not considered as problematic.

This view contrasts with the perspectives and priorities which would reflect those ascribing to a constructivist model of learning. Within research, any attempt to claim objectivity is considered flawed by the belief that actions cannot be reduced to measurements. Contexts and perspectives cannot be assumed to be constant and stable. As Gorman (1977: 123) states, objective truth, sought through scientific exactitude 'is built on subjectivism falsely "reduced" to physical objectivity by social convention'. Subjectivity is therefore inevitable. Schratz and Walker (1995) state that the main purpose of trying to seek objectivity is not so much in the research tools and processes used as in the struggle to be free from prejudice and bias, and is largely defined by 'power' interests in research and scientific communities. All research, whether objective or subjective, involves social activity and therefore involves some level of political action. However, under the guise of objectivity, political disputes or priorities are defended by isolating the specific technical problem of knowledge and isolating any bias or unwanted interference. The resulting 'evidence' forms the basis for generalisation, whether for political purposes or for theoretical status. It allows for the abstraction of theory from practice, permitting knowledge to be devoid of ownership, construction, time and place. In the context of formal national and standardised assessments, are assumptions that bias and prejudice can be eliminated. Knowledge can be reduced and generalised in order to provide evidence for developing and executing political agendas. Shifting the research paradigm so that subjectivity is recognised as inevitable and is part of the research agenda requires a very different approach serving different purposes.

As in the case of constructivism, much of post-modernist critique has argued against prestructured and agreed forms of knowledge. Without such bodies of established knowledge any form of measurement or understanding must move away from rational and logocentric approaches. Validity and certainty are considered as forms of representation which must be challenged. Lather (1993: 677) claimed:

> Contrary to dominant validity practices where the rhetorical nature of scientific claims is masked with methodological assurances, a strategy of ironic validity proliferates forms, recognising that they are rhetorical and without foundation, post-epistemic, lacking epistemological support.

If a post-modern view is advanced in relation to the status of knowledge and the search for truth, there is the obvious objection that everything is 'up for grabs'. With such a view all is in disarray and there can never be consensus. Indeed, in Lyotard's (1984) terms dissensus is the inevitable outcome. However, recognising that scientific rationality is problematic does not necessarily outlaw all forms of consensus; and recognising individual views and perspectives does not permit common understandings. However, to move towards recognising these different views requires acknowledgement of the complex, the irregular, the multidimensional necessarily involving relational and interdisciplinary dialogues and discourses.

As part of an agenda which seeks to understand a phenomenon, whether in a broader research sense or in the realms of assessment, the processes of engagement as well as the outcomes will relate to the view of knowledge and truth promoted. Striving for generalisability and abstraction is not the ultimate goal. Schratz and Walker (1995: 105) suggest that research should seek to prevent generalisations. Our natural human tendencies, they claim, indicate that we all too readily try to generalise. A key function of research, therefore, should be to slow down, or even block this process. Certainly within the context of assessments the task of summative assessment, which calls for generalisations to be made, requires careful consideration. Attempts to over-focus such assessments will provide only limited information which may not adequately reflect a pupil's learning. Seeking to explore learning in a variety of contexts and to delay trying to make summative judgements too quickly, or even (in the case of STs) instantly, may encourage the extent of pupil learning to be more representatively portrayed.

The research design required here would need to explore possible bias, cater for differing contexts and recognise the possible influence of individual preference and priority. Any notion that a 'formula' research design could be used must be questioned. Rather than moving through the five categories of research design which Cizek (op. cit.) presented in a linear way the categories would not be so clearly designed or so rigidly structured. With a focus on formative assessment, the possible influence of a research paradigm on explaining and developing assessment practice, is an important link to pursue.

Formative assessment as qualitative research

The mutual enhancement of teaching and learning in the classroom has been claimed to be the prime purpose of formative assessment. If processes of learning are complex involving the unique interpretation of meaning through complex cognitive constructs, attempts to gain some understanding of learning will not be easy. Any attempt to assess such learning will require cooperation and participation from both pupil and teacher. The scope and scale of these assessments will be dependent on the extent to which learning can be demonstrated and articulated. Furthermore, as judgements and interpretations are made by those involved in the processes, learning will be influenced. Accordingly, the process and product of assessment are not easily dichotomised in this complex relationship.

As with assessment in the national public arena there is a concern with credibility and reliability in the more local arena of formative assessment. Here the status of these concepts will be very different from those within the objective 'camp'. The reason for this will be associated with differences between the purposes and products of assessment. As part of the assessment process the educational context and substance of learning is regarded as complex and socially influenced. Rather than attempting to simplify and reduce the processes of learning and achievement so that notional insights are gained, possibilities for interpretation and understanding need to be maximised. The range of evidence available will thus be broad.

Gipps et al. (1995) examined the impact of Key Stage 1 national assessments on teachers' existing practices. They found that teachers (prior to the introduction of STs) claimed that their assessments were fairly intuitive. This finding concurred with the PACE study which spanned the early 1990s. As the national pressure for raised standards based on national assessment evidence mounted, teachers' views of best assessment practice shifted. By the end of the PACE research teachers were clear that the assessments 'that mattered' were those which were based on clearly defined and interpreted evidence. This view is highlighted by Torrance and Pryor (1998: 34): they explored teachers' views that teacher assessment, at a classroom level, 'had come to be regarded by them as a rather "low-level" intuitive activity, which they were unable to organise into a coherent theoretical alternative to the incremental evidence gathering which they thought was required for teacher assessment'. Intuition thus seemed no longer acceptable and has been marginalised from the realms of acceptability. Yet if formative assessment is to exist in classrooms based on daily learning events intuition will feature. Ignoring it is not the answer. Examining it, however, may help.

Atkinson and Claxton (2000) present the 'intuitive practitioner'. H/she is a rehabilitation of Schon's concept of the reflective practitioner. Schon (1983: 5) recognised the limitations of 'practice implicit in the artistic intuitive processes which can be brought by practitioners to divergent contexts which face instability, uniqueness and value conflict'. Rather than teachers being reflective practitioners who reflect on their actions, their reflection is *in* the action – in the process of acting. It is therefore, to some extent considered as intuitive. The sense of immediacy is an essential characteristic here. Additionally, reference to any theory may not be fully reasoned and conscious. In Claxton's (2000: 40) terms intuition is a different 'way' of knowing. It is the immediate apprehension, without the intervention of the reasoning process. It can function within simple or complex contexts. In recognising the complexity of classroom environments, the process of intuition may well be a process which permits 'a way' of knowing that does not seek to eliminate and reduce complexity but work with it. Bruner claimed that

> intuitive thinking characteristically does not advance in careful, well-planned steps. Indeed, it tends to involve manoeuvres based seemingly on perception of the total problem. The thinker arrives at an answer, which may be right or wrong, with little, if any awareness of the process by which he reached it.
>
> (Bruner 1960 57–58)

If the process of intuition features in classroom assessment its methods are not transparent. Claxton (2000: 40) attempts to define some parameters of intuition by detailing six 'ways' of knowing which could be intuitive:

- Expertise – the unreflective execution of intricate skilled performance.
- Implicit learning – the acquisition of such expertise by non-conscious or non-conceptual means.
- Judgement – making accurate decisions and categories without, at the time, being able to explain or justify them.
- Sensitivity – to heighten attentiveness, but conscious and non-conscious, to details of a situation.
- Creativity – the use of incubation and reverie to enhance problem solving.
- Rumination – the process of 'chewing the cud' of experience in order to extract its meanings and its implications.

Each seems to have direct application to formative assessment.

Expertise: research which focused on teachers' assessment practices before National Curriculum and assessment requirements indicated how their ability to make assessment judgements was a product of expertise. This often could not be clearly defined and was usually linked to experience (Gipps *et al.* 1995). With the advent of more formalised and standardised assessment procedures in relation to national summative assessment frameworks teachers seem to have been less concerned with the details of formative assessment judgements based on their established expertise but on implementing assessment which they hope will satisfy external accountability demands (Harlen and James 1997).

Implicit learning: as teachers engage with pupils through the teaching process they develop a range of knowledge about their learning. Formative assessment continually results in a range of information being assimilated often subconsciously.

Judgement: the information assimilated is used to inform the many judgements that teachers make about pupils and their own teaching that are ongoing and enable the momentum of teaching and learning to continue.

Sensitivity: the teacher is able to be context specific, being sensitive to particular needs without preparing or preconsidering responses. Similarly, as teaching and learning progress novel and/or alternative approaches will be generated and created in response to pupils' progress in order to engage and motivate children.

Creativity enables the tool of teaching to be sharp and direct in a way which is spontaneous but based on intuitive judgements about teaching and learning. Teachers' skills are partly driven by consideration of experience both conscious and sub-conscious. Reflecting on successes and mistakes enables the practitioner to intervene more appropriately.

Rumination, at an intuitive or conscious level, requires self-evaluation and assessment. (This is discussed in detail in Chapters 6 and 7.)

Broadfoot (2000: 201), in explicitly exploring assessment and intuition, argues that 'what is urgently needed now is the beginnings of an active search for a more humanistic, even intuitive, approach to educational assessment'. In this vein, teachers carrying out formative assessment are continually making judgements about children's responses to learning. To some extent these will be related to teachers' own mental and cultural models of learning development and achievement – despite attempts in England and Wales to standardise perceptions. Teachers' own interpretations of national requirements as well as their views on pupils' needs will inevitably differ. Collaboration and discussion can offer some scope for consensus. Yet, when the complexity of learning is considered, precise statements would seem to offer only oversimplistic statements.

As in the case of qualitative research, parameters must be explored and explained rather than set and then disregarded. Competing, influencing and even conflicting issues and areas should be acknowledged and considered rather than marginalised. The dynamic relationship between teacher and pupil should be explored and not reduced to a simplistic input/output model. The role of the person being assessed cannot therefore, be as 'object' but as 'participant'. Such a view calls for radical reconsideration of teaching and learning through assessment and of teacher/pupil relationships within all areas.

Aspects of research and thinking in assessment are reviewed as starting points for a new direction in formative assessment. These embrace the nature and role of assessment feedback which relates to the teacher/pupil dynamic which can be developed in formative assessment.

New directions in formative assessment

If learning, which is identified as involving complex structuring and restructuring of information through interactions and experience, is to advance, the interface between assessment and learning must inevitably be dynamic, complex and collaborative. At a simplistic level, one of the key features of assessment which will impact on learning is the feedback which a pupil receives from the assessment process. Learning can only advance if pupils are able and willing to act on the information given or to have constructed it already for themselves. Harlen and James (1997) highlight the importance of feedback which shows pupils how to close the gap between their own work and the curriculum aims or targets presented. Sadler (1998) points out that it should not be assumed that pupils will know what to do with the feedback they are given. Black and Wiliam (1998), in their extensive review of formative assessment illustrate from recent research the forms and effects of feedback. Its potential catalytic role in transforming learning is highlighted. However, its limitations related to pupils' willingness and ability to engage with the learning process are critical. Sadler (1989) highlights the importance of pupils being able to make judgements about their own learning. The role and function of pupil self-assessment is presented as an essential feature of formative assessment. The processes through which pupils need to progress in order to close the gap between their achievements and their potential achievements requires more development and examination; this forms the focus of Chapter 6. For feedback to have the desired impact the communication between the teacher and the pupil needs to act as 'scaffolding' for learning.

Conclusion

Despite the analysis of national assessment systems being identified as increasingly focused on summative judgements used for account-ability, the scope, and indeed the necessity, for teachers' own formative assessment is advanced. Building on the analysis of learning theories in the previous chapter, this chapter has offered both contextual and development factors for formative assessment. The following three chapters explore a range of possibilities for developing classroom assessment practices. They are located within the demands of the changing national context and, indeed, in the case of Chapter 4, exploit national testing requirements for formative means. More importantly they seek to develop a deeper understanding of assessment and learning which recognises and seeks to build on the dynamics of learning.

Constructing learning contexts from testing regimes

'The individual in contemporary society is not so much described by tests as constructed by them'

(Hanson 2000: 68)

Introduction

The role and function of national tests has been discussed within a national policy context. Its regulatory function has been identified together with the extent to which it has steered curriculum developments (Chapters 2 and 3). Data and analysis from the PACE project (Primary Assessment, Curriculum and Experience: Pollard *et al.* 1994), which explored changes since the introduction of the National Curriculum, drew on notions of power and authority. The foundation for this view stemmed from Bernstein's theories in which he advocated that assessment was one of the purest forms of pedagogic control. In identifying the shift from a competency orientation in primary education to a performance orientation the changes and emphasis in national assessment have had a significant impact. (Competency orientation – in which the individual is identified as active and creative in the construction of meaning and practice combined with an educational approach which emphasises who we are rather than who we might become. Performance orientation – emphasises a particular outcome from an individual which is linked to regularised learning texts and contexts judged through specific assessments.) As Broadfoot and Pollard (2000: 21) assert two fundamental discourses can be drawn from the PACE study – 'regulatory' and 'instructional' discourses. Regulatory discourses relate to the creation and maintenance of social order and control whereas instructional discourses embrace the processes and practices of pedagogy. It is becoming increasingly clear that developments in national assessment have impacted significantly on both these discourses. Of particular note are the promotion of league tables, target setting and benchmarking which, together with the drive for raising standards measured through assessment, are used to judge school effectiveness. These regulative discourses influence social order, social relations as well as social identity. Additionally, the change in the form, structure and language of assessment, through instructional discourse, influences the nature of both teaching and learning. The power of assessment to influence education so markedly is attracting considerable and deserved attention. Yet, the role of teachers in influencing the processes is given rather less attention. Although the instructional and regulative discourses have been greatly altered through national changes in assessment, the potential, as well as the actual role of teachers in mediating these changes seems crucial (Pollard *et al.* 1994). In this respect Dann and Simco (2000: 39) argue that 'what appears to be tight national description does not, in effect, lead to consistent, even patterns of change in classrooms'. Indeed the attempt by central government to enforce a culture of compliance will, in fact, lead to a culture of mediation (p.38). By both recognising and developing the view that the teachers' role need not be completely subservient to driving policy agendas, this chapter considers two strands. First, that teachers do have considerable control in classrooms and can engage in creative reinterpretation of policy directives and guidance in the midst of severe regulatory pressures. Second, that within a performance orientation and all that seems to engender, particularly in relation to underlying notions of learning, alternative practices and priorities can be advanced. This offers the potential to challenge the popular notion that the outcomes of 'performativity', for both teachers and pupils, provide a legitimating function which defines success and failure.

Context

The chapter focuses on Year 6 (pupils age 10–11). This year group has, since 1995, been subjected to changing pressures caused by the introduction of end of KS 2 national tests. The results of a small-scale inquiry into the nature of some of these changes is included in the chapter alongside evidence from national sources. By establishing the nature of perceived requirements and the changes which have been implemented, the chapter seeks to identify ways in which the national demands are met as well as contextualised in the classroom. By drawing on the priorities and principles for constructive learning (Chapter 2) this chapter considers some theoretical and policy foundations as well as some strategies for supporting pupils for successful Standard Test (ST) completion through constructive learning frameworks and experiences.

This focus on Year 6 is linked to the emerging trends related to the preparation of pupils for the STs. Evaluation of the Key Stage 2 tests, since their requirement in 1995, indicates that preparation procedures for national tests has increasingly become part of the Year 6 experience. The School Curriculum and Assessment Authority (SCAA) report for 1995 states that between 78 and 83 per cent of teachers gave advice on test techniques (range indicates differences in core subject areas). In 1996 this rose to 93 per cent, and in 1997 the statement that 'in almost all schools, children were prepared for the tests' (QCA: 1998) was included. Additionally, it was indicated in the evaluation in 1995 that between 49 and 55 per cent of teachers used the previous year's pilot tests for practice (some variation in use relating to different subject areas). In 1996 the report indicated that 71 per cent of teachers used tests from the previous year. In 1995 between 37 and 43 per cent of teachers used other types of test materials for ST preparation. In 1996 this increased to 68 per cent. Curriculum revision was used in 1995 by many teachers in the areas of mathematics (60 per cent) and science (74 per cent) – no percentages for English. In 1996, 85 per cent of teachers indicated that they undertook curriculum revision with their children (no individual core subject data).

This information from 1995 and 1996, together with the 1997 statement (offering no substance to what constituted 'preparation' but indicating that it was now an expected national practice), indicated changing practices by Year 6 teachers aimed at preparing pupils for Standard Tests. The categories used to identify preparation practices were not discussed or seen as complex in any way. No regard was given to the ways in which these were conceptualised or delivered. Thus, the complex ways in which teaching, learning and assessment were being changed in this context were not examined.

Since the compulsory testing at the end of Key Stage 2 began, little research has been published on its impact in classrooms. However, Clarke's (1996) study highlights some responses to the first year of the tests. Here, teachers identified a preparation period in which they carried out the following practices (in order of frequency): science revision of factual knowledge; mathematics revision; timed essays; previous test papers; spelling tests and dictations; comprehension exercises; familiarisation with format. About 40 per cent of the teachers in this study indicated that they would spend more time on preparation in the following year. Interestingly, Clarke stated that when teachers were asked if they had changed their teaching style, the majority of them at Key Stage 2 said that they had not. (This contrasted with the Key Stage 1 teachers in Clarke's study who had already had three years' experience with national tests. Clarke notes that, with more experience, Key Stage 2 teachers may well have a different response.) Evidence from the final phase of the PACE study suggested that the impact of external and overt testing was great. Practising for tests was clearly evident. More specifically, by the end of the study pupils' perception and awareness of testing was significant (double that in previous years). The children had interpreted the learning climate to be performance driven. Accordingly, they were avoiding challenge and had a low tolerance for ambiguity since they were increasingly keen to do whatever would gain them most credit (Pollard and Triggs 2000). They had perceptively adopted certain priorities in the curriculum which were related to the focus of the tests and their eagerness to succeed in them.

From the published evidence available, the amount of time spent on preparation for Standard Tests, and the nature of such preparation, are not clearly examined. The impact of 'preparation', however, has already received comment. Clarke points out that preparation has affected pupils' learning so that pupils 'learn how to do a test' and 'retain knowledge for a short period'. She indicates that the way in which pupils learn science has changed so that facts are now emphasised at the expense of experimentation and investigation. Curiously, the inevitable change in teaching style alluded to here was not mentioned by the KS 2 teachers in her study. Furthermore, the impact of preparation was recognised by SCAA in the Key Stage 2 evaluations in 1996 and by QCA in 1998a. Overall, trends in national tests at KS 2 have shown improvements by pupils – in maths and English. (Changes in test paper design to make the science tests papers in 1996 more challenging at level 5 than they were in 1995, does not allow improvement to be adequately explained from 1995 to 1996 in science.) Improvements, in English and maths, are evident from the evaluation reports. SCAA (1996: 2, 11 and 1997: 2, 16) state that for both English and maths, improvements between 1995 and 1997 were due to increased familiarity with the demands of the tests as well as real improvements in children's standards of achievement. Linking improvement with familiarity, in this context, identifies a connection between preparation and outcome, although it is not clear on the relative levels of familiarity implied for teachers and pupils. In seeking to gain greater understanding of the nature of preparation, attention is now focused on the type of knowledge which is tested at the end of Key Stage 2 tests.

The Year 6 context

Since the early days of the implementation of the National Curriculum, review and modification have resulted in some changes to the structure as well as a reduction in content. This slimming down of the curriculum (post-Dearing) and the move away from levelled statements of attainments to level descriptors may have improved manageability. More recent challenges to the National Curriculum, particularly related to primary education, highlighted pupils' standards in basic numeracy and literacy skills were not high enough. Teachers contended that the curriculum demands of the foundation subjects left inadequate time for proper treatment of the core subjects. The literacy and numeracy hours, introduced into primary classrooms, outlined structures for teaching and class-room organisation rather than just curriculum content. The 'unity of purpose' which, according to Kenneth Baker (then Secretary of State for Education), was to be the foundation for the National Curriculum seemed to be shifting to embrace unity of practice. With the 'lift' on the foundation subjects between 1998 and 2000 the impact on the knowledge base of primary pedagogy was re-focused. With Curriculum 2000 being fully implemented in September 2001, the priority of the core subjects elevated certain forms of knowledge and left the 'non-core' subjects to a formalised status that was encapsulated by the 'prioritise, reduce and combine' philosophy which was promoted during their temporary lifting prior to Curriculum 2000 (QCA: 1998b). (In the period leading to Curriculum 2000, existing foundation subject requirements were lifted and teachers were invited to teach these subjects by selecting aspects of them on the basis of priority, reduction and combination.)

In a public education system there needs to be a form of account-ability which indicates that the nation's investment in teachers and education yields the highest possible educational achievements. Prescribing a National Curriculum, then assessing pupils' achievements in relation to it – through national testing in the core subjects and teacher assessment in the foundation subjects – is the current means of fulfilling this. The intended combination of teacher assessment with standard assessment tasks identified by TGAT, has been completely abandoned in the core subjects (Black 1998). Accordingly, it seems that input into non-tested areas is not valued, and is marginalised. Is accountability the overarching aim of the curriculum? What of the other aims – progression, continuity, breadth and balance, individual challenges for all pupils? Elliott (1998: 31) warns of the severe limitations of this objectives model and he offers three main objections to it:

> The implementation of a national curriculum constructed through an objectives model and representing knowledge as unproblematic (1), as an individual rather than social achievement (2), and as something acquired by progressively moving through higher and higher levels of abstraction (3), will suppress rather than enhance the intellectual development of the majority of children in our schools. As a vision of what is involved in providing the mass of the citizenry with equality of educational opportunity, it is seriously flawed.
>
> (My numbering)

With the aims of education being pushed towards achievement of objectives in a public arena, it seems that the success of primary education is being judged at the end of Year 6. Pupils' results thus contribute towards creating national, local and school level pictures of achievement. The stakes being high and becoming higher, schools seek to ensure that their pupils achieve the best possible results in the areas of national interest being tested. Previous experiences of high-stakes national tests both in this country and the United States highlight likely trends which are useful for comparative and illustrative purposes.

Measurement Driven Instruction (MDI) offers one example. Gipps (1994: 32), drawing from Popham, explains MDI:

> When a high-stakes test, because of the important contingencies associated with the students' performance, influences the instructional programme that prepares students for the tests.

Popham (in Gipps) identifies the necessary conditions for its success as follows:

1. Criterion references tests must be used to clarify the skills and knowledge that will be measured, and to provide the instructional tasks for teachers.
2. Non-trivial knowledge and skills must be measured.
3. A manageable number of skills or objectives must be measured, with the lower ones subsumed by the higher level skills.
4. Instructional clarity must come from the targets, so that teachers can use the targets or objectives for planning teaching.
5. Instructional support, useful teaching materials, and suggestions for how skills can be taught must be part of the programme.

(Gipps 1994: 33)

Such conditions are to a great extent in place or near to being in place in England and Wales – (point 5 being most recently serviced by the instructional support from the literacy and numeracy hours). At Key Stage 2, with five years of testing now undertaken, along with an additional two years of pilot testing, a legacy of past papers is emerging, as well as evaluation reports, which include advice for future teaching and learning. In principle these offer teachers further help in gaining greater clarity in understanding how teaching can most effectively address the demands of the objectives. The interest in the CD-ROM past test papers (2000) available (for a fee) from QCA demonstrates the formalisation and recognition of test paper practice. With the possibility of high-stakes tests which are carefully constructed to measure specified skills in a way which gives explicit instructional goals to teachers and objective information to the public, Madaus (1988, in Gipps 1994) claims that MDI can have perceived benefits, mainly that improved pupil results are assumed to indicate better education. Madaus's seven principles outline an intrepid path for MDI. One certainly shares his sentiment in principle 6 which highlights the limitations of society treating test results as the major goal of schooling, rather than just one of many possible indicators of achievement. His seven principles are summarised below:

1. The power of tests is founded on people's perceptions of them. If they are believed to be 'high stakes' then they will be.
2. If the test is used for social decision making it is likely to corrupt the process it is intended to assess.

3. If important decisions are based on test results then teachers will teach to the test.
4. Where high stakes tests operate a tradition of past exams will develop.
5. Teachers will look carefully at the type of questions being asked and adjust their teaching to address these forms;
6. If tests are the main or only source of making future educational or life choices then society will tend to see test results as the most important goal and outcome of schooling.
7. High stakes testing shifts control of the curriculum to those who design the tests.

(Adapted from Madaus 1988, in Gipps 1994: 34–7)

Experiences of testing in England and Wales also merit attention even if they are from the previous century. Following the Report of the Newcastle Commission in 1861, the Revised Code was implemented. In an attempt to extend 'sound and cheap elementary education for all classes' the Commission called for all children to have a sound grasp of the 3Rs. It stated:

> However good the influence of the elementary school may be, it has failed with respect to every child who having attended it for a certain time has not learned these things perfectly.
>
> (Vol. 1: 157)

This alluded to the desire for all children to achieve a particular standard which is also currently evident in the expectations accompanying progression through the National Curriculum. The degree of competence to be attained ('perfection'), however, may seem a little ambitious and defy easy consensus for certifying achievement! The stakes were certainly high, since a teacher's salary was dependent on the standards achieved. Accordingly, as is likely with high-stakes tests, teachers tried to ensure that their pupils succeeded. (A scenario which may not be too far away if the talked about higher salaried 'super-teachers' were to be created.) As Matthew Arnold, an inspector during this period, wrote in his general report for 1869:

> The school examinations in view of payment by results are, as I have said, a game of mechanical contrivance in which teachers will and must more and more learn how to beat us.
>
> (Arnold 1910: 125)

He claimed that the curriculum had been narrowed and that results were merely an 'illusion' of achievement since pupils were often unable to perform the same skills in different contexts. So important was a pupil's performance that F.G. Gould (1880), a great and humane teacher of the era, declared that he felt a measure of relief when one of his 'backward' boys died of bronchitis; for his death would make one failure the less.

High-stakes tests, whatever the context, seem to have resulted in a narrowing of the curriculum to reflect the demands of the tests, and the use of teaching practices which are considered most beneficial to successful test performance. The notion of 'teaching to the test' is increasingly prevalent. It may well be that the legacies of the past have profound influences here. Yet it is important to remember that the National Curriculum was revolutionary in its time and is different from other types of previously tested curricula. The type of learning tested and the ways in which this learning is achieved merits more specific discussion before the teaching implications for Year 6 tests are examined.

Testing learning

So far discussion in Chapter 2 has indicated concern over an objectives model which identifies testable knowledge for external accountability. In this chapter the particular emphasis of this model within Year 6 is advanced. The aim of this section is to explore the type of knowledge which recent Key Stage 2 national tests in English, maths and science have examined, and the learning pupils need in order to be successful in these tests. Within the context of national testing, the emerging picture is far from simple. Certainly dismissive comments and hasty conclusions are no substitute for carefully considered research which is minimal in this field.

Most of the items in the national tests require pupils to apply knowledge, to interpret it in new contexts or to explain their understanding of it. The worst fears about national testing previously identified, which anticipated narrowly focused tests measuring superficial understanding and the recall of facts, do not seem to be evident in most aspects of the core subjects which are tested at the end of Key Stage 2. There are some exceptions, however, particularly in science such as the labelling of parts of a flower or parts of the body, and the use of 'thin' skills such as handwriting in English. There are some exceptions, which require the recall of factual knowledge – particularly in science. The concepts and knowledge which pupils need to know are clearly set out in the National Curriculum, whereas the contexts and nature of interconnections of such knowledge and understanding of it are not. This allows teachers' professional scope in the classroom to structure and deliver their teaching. Pupils may understand concepts in different ways and at different levels which need to be addressed in both teaching and assessment. For example, at a simplistic level, a teacher may assess a pupil as understanding the concept of subtraction within a series of lessons based on it. However, that child may fail to select subtraction as the correct operation for solving a mathematical problem in a new context. What, then, are we to assess about such a pupil's understanding of subtraction? If the concept of subtraction were to be fully tested, then several examples requiring different types of use and application would need to be included. Understanding cannot be identified as all or nothing from one or two similar examples. The two end of Key Stage 2 test papers (levels 3–5) in maths provide a variety of examples for pupils to show their understanding in different ways. In science also, some of the concepts are probed in more than one way. In the end of Key Stage 2 English tests, pupils' understanding of a text is assessed through different types of written material which seek different types of understanding and interpretation. (It is evidently more difficult to cross-check the level of pupils' understanding in this area since different examples draw on different concepts and experiences which are not necessarily the specific focus of the questions.) Thus, by using questions which require different types of application of the same concept many areas of learning are assessed in complex ways through the national tests. As Wiliam (2001) forcibly argues, the number of questions which would need to be asked in order for the national tests results to have a meaningful level of reliability would require each test to be about 30 hours long! Failing this, the results will have a margin of error that renders the level allocations as fairly meaningless. Unfortunately, in addition to this, the relationship between the learning assessed and the way results are recorded and communicated is dominated by summative purposes, giving no specific information about aspects of learning within the attainment targets. Nevertheless, test papers may be carefully examined when they are returned to schools. In order to prepare pupils for what might be tested, revision should address all possible concepts included on the syllabus (programmes of study) and ways in which these might be probed.

This should lead to a broad rather than narrow context for teaching and learning in test preparation in identified curriculum areas.

A further issue related to the knowledge which is tested concerns marking structures. It seems that the questions posed may not necessarily reveal the full extent of the knowledge and understanding being assessed. Questions that are probing and seeking to establish how concepts are applied or how thinking is connected may not be marked in a way which actually assesses such learning. The STs are accompanied with explicit details of marking which imposes a rigorous structure on the way answers can be interpreted. In their endeavour to be rigorous and standardised, answers need to conform to certain views. To illustrate, Ray (2001) explores the way in which children are deemed successful, or not so successful, in the KS 2 writing task. She claims that the writing test is not so much concerned with writing style but with writing structure – mainly through correct use of punctuation. Both teachers' and pupils' understanding of such an agenda seems important in ensuring that any preparation is adequately focused.

Clearly then, the ways in which pupils learn the contents of the programmes of study are important if they are to be successful in the tests. Exploring the relationship between knowledge, understanding and application in this process evokes considerable interest and poses a considerable challenge. As already indicated, a main focus of the Standard Tests is on the application of concepts and knowledge to new examples and contexts. This requires pupils to decode and solve problems as part of the tests. However, more than this, pupils are required to give reasons for their answers, reflecting on the thinking they have used. This requires a deeper level of understanding. In order to be successful in this process they should have memorised some information, be able to solve problems and demonstrate understanding. The last two abilities, however, need to be demonstrated conventionally and within the established parameters identified by the test constructors. They are, therefore, judged in relation to specific objectives but are not narrowly focused on one particular type of learning which is usually associated with testing (memorisation). Stevenson and Palmer (1994) identify three types of learning, which in the context of this chapter, reflect the essential learning Year 6 pupils need to demonstrate at the end of Key Stage 2 national tests.

Understanding – involves integrating new material with prior knowledge, but it also goes beyond simple integration to a two-way process of evaluation, in which prior knowledge is used to assess how well the new material has been understood, and the new material is used to evaluate and modify pre-existing knowledge. Prior knowledge is thus a key ingredient . . .

Problem solving – involves discovery, or being told, the solution to a problem and how to arrive at that solution. Once the problem and how to reach it is known, the problem can be repeated many times until it can be retrieved from memory automatically, and the individual steps in the problem-solving process become part of implicit knowledge. Without the involvement of prior knowledge to give significance to the task, problem solving becomes an end in itself . . .

Memorization – involves consolidation, through revision of (newly understood) material until it too can be automatically retrieved from memory without conscious effort. Unfortunately, as was the case with problem solving, memorization too often is seen as a learning goal in itself and material is memorized with few, if any, attempts to understand it. Material learned in this way may be superficially integrated with prior knowledge, but since the two-way process of evaluation is not applied, understanding is also superficial.

(Stevenson and Palmer 1994: 178)

Stevenson and Palmer emphasise the importance of understanding which they claim may not occur in successful problem solving and memorisation learning since it involves a process of evaluating pre-existing knowledge. Interestingly, in their summary of memorisation, they indicate that this process is undertaken with 'newly understood' material. If this is the case, then their following contention, stating that there may be little or only superficial 'understanding' as a result of memorisation, is contradictory. My use of brackets is used to indicate that memorisation may be of any material so that it is automatically retrievable and may not involve the process of understanding in the way defined here.

If pupils are to gain levels 3, 4, 5 or 6 at Key Stage 2 they will need to demonstrate all three types of learning – understanding being the most difficult, requiring prior knowledge and metacognitive skills [evaluating the process of thinking/learning] and most likely to demarcate achievement of the higher levels. If pupils are to successfully demonstrate their learning Stevenson and Palmer (1994: 180) identify three crucial principles.

1. The activation of prior knowledge is crucial for new learning.
2. The learner's motivation determines how much effort s/he chooses to invest.
3. Learning through understanding depends on metacognitive skills.

Much of our teaching in primary schools may be considered fragmentary in that several unconnected topics/themes are introduced and developed over planned periods of time, some topics are sometimes revisited and further developed in later years. Pressures of time and content mean that pupils are often not able to linger on material in a way which allows them to make appropriate connections with previous learning or to reflect, consolidate, repeat and revise so that their understanding can develop.

In trying to identify more coherent themes across curriculum boundaries there have been attempts to develop cross-curriculum skills in teaching. Developing pupils' thinking skills is a particular example with relevance in the context of this discussion. Lipman (1991) and Fisher (1990), as two influential proponents, have advanced a range of teaching materials designed to promote higher order thinking skills which they claim are not adequately covered in the curriculum. Their techniques are not specifically drawn from subject specific areas but teach thinking skills in a way which they believe are transferable across the curriculum. Any knowledge content is seen, by these proponents, only as a vehicle for developing thinking skills. Clear links can be seen here with Piaget's work. For Piaget assumed that when a particular form of reasoning or thinking developed during one of the stages of his model of cognitive development it could be applied in different contexts. Neo-Piagetian writing, however, raises some objections here; notably that pupils can display different forms of development of particular concepts and still be classified as being at the same stage in Piaget's model. Piaget's unilinear model of progression is often more cautiously considered in terms of a multilinear process (Crahay 1996). If Stevenson and Palmer's contention is upheld, understanding requires prior knowledge and therefore thinking skills cannot be developed in isolation from knowledge. Thus, attempts to promote pupils' understanding by teaching higher order thinking skills as a separate subject seems unlikely to be able to help pupils' learning.

Further support for this view is offered by Crahay (1996: 58) who claims:

Intellectual processes cannot be defined independently of the knowledge or content to be mastered or the problems to be solved. More specifically still, there is no point in defining intellectual processes or aptitudes which the pupils should have at their command, without specifying the knowledge or situations in which this process should be applied.

The notion that skills can be learnt and then successfully applied in a different context is therefore seen as problematic. It assumes that a set of rules or procedures have been learnt which can be separated from content. The assumption that those concepts included can be generalised to reflect the whole of the subject remains uncertain. Recent government interest in the development of pupils' thinking skills seems to indicate that these should be taught separately. The interest, however, has no rationale, and features only in general terms in the introductory section which highlights skills across the curriculum (DfEE/QCA 1999: 22).

An additional area for concern is that the application of knowledge is examined not only conceptually, in relation to prior knowledge, but also in terms of the semantics of understanding. The way a problem is presented can greatly influence the way in which it is decoded. Subsequently this may influence the selection of a procedure which it is believed will allow the correct solution to be found. Applying knowledge or problem solving will therefore be affected by prior knowledge and experience: the way in which these are structured and the speed in which they can be accessed from the memory are also significant and also needed to be briefly outlined.

In exploring processes of learning, it can already be seen that understanding, problem solving and memorisation are not completely distinctive processes. Memorisation, the most mechanical type of learning, is required for the higher order processes or problem solving and understanding. What needs to be distinguished is memory which allows information to be retained and recalled and the memory which synthesises knowledge so that it can be recalled and applied. The short-term memory (working memory) processes new knowledge and information so that connections can be made with existing information that can then be stored in the long-term memory. Frequent repetition and new presentations of knowledge help the working memory to make a range of different links to existing knowledge and to structure it. Since the working memory has a limited capacity, with a possible consequence of becoming easily 'blocked', its most efficient use needs to be recognised. Crahay (1996) indicates the importance of the structure of knowledge in the long-term memory in aiding the effective functioning of the working memory. He claims that the short-term memory processes new information in the structured forms in which they exist in the long-term memory. Thus, the more highly structured the items of knowledge are in the long-term memory, the more effective the working memory becomes, enhancing individuals' cognitive skills. Furthermore, if the information in the long-term memory is automatic then responses can be even more easily activated without overloading the working memory (Ericsson and Oliver 1995: 51).

Automatic responses, however, do need to be recognised with caution since, if they are carried out almost unconsciously, errors can easily be made as incorrect decoding of a problem can trigger the wrong response or trigger a response which does not cater for the question posed. Such processes will not serve pupils well in school. However, as a way of helping pupils with an initial response which can subsequently be further examined, they are invaluable. As knowledge is related to previous knowledge through different contexts, in a way which enables the long-term memory to become more structured and organised through the connections made with the working memory, learning advances. Children will increasingly be able to solve problems and answer questions as they construct meanings and frames of reference. Yet for understanding to develop they will need the metacognitive skills that require reflection and evaluation of procedures used. In recognising the range of learning that needs to be demonstrated for success on national tests and the complexities related to the developing of such learning, how can teachers adequately prepare pupils for the challenges of Year 6 tests?

Classroom pragmatics from the perspectives of a focus group

It seems particularly pertinent to explore the extent to which teachers establish their practice in order to achieve what they deem to be best for their pupils within the performance culture of STs. In an attempt to temper the 'what might be' (so far explored in this chapter) with the 'what is' (in Year 6 classrooms), some evidence from a small focus group study is included. The data included are intended to be illustrative, providing a glimpse into the way a small group of Year 6 teachers shape and structure the Year 6 experience. It is included to help ground the discussion in classroom realities and to explore the ways in which teachers perceive and structure the task of ST revision.

Eleven teachers were involved in the focus group during 1998. Ten of these teachers had taught Year 6 for at least two years in the period following the introduction of Key Stage 2 national tests in 1995. All the teachers were in schools which were part of the primary teacher training partnership at Keele University and had expressed an interest in joining a small Year 6 project following an invitation to all schools (with Year 6 classes) in the partnership. Seven of the eleven teachers had taught Year 6 in all four years of the STs. Drawing on their experiences of having taught Year 6 previously, ten of the teachers indicated their agreement with the statements shown in Figure 4.1.

All eleven teachers were invited to select one of the statements shown in Figure 4.2 to reflect their feelings of teaching Year 6.

Given that the nature of Year 6 teaching had changed, less than half of the teachers stated that they found this new type of teaching became easier with practice. Consolidation over time was thus a feature for some of these teachers. Interestingly, however, for over half of the teachers, the task of preparing for national tests was not becoming easier with practice. Perhaps there has been insufficient time for consolidation. Perhaps the variation in the tests each year,

Preparing pupils for STs becomes easier with practice	4
Less time has been spent preparing pupils because I am more focused in my approach	0
More time is spent preparing pupils for STs since I have realised how much is needed if they are to be successful	6
I have managed to merge teaching and ST preparation more effectively so that they are not clearly distinct	1
I have sensed a greater pressure, because of result publication, to make 'preparation' more of a priority	8
KS 2 tests affect teaching throughout KS 2	3

Figure 4.1 The perceived pressure of teaching Year 6.

My teaching seems to be hijacked by the demands of KS 2 tests	1
The demands of the KS 2 tests are significant but I try to put them into perspective	10
I don't see any tension between my usual teaching and the demands of Standard Tests	0

Figure 4.2 Teachers' responses to teaching Year 6.

as well as the altering emphases in the core curriculum, have not promoted sufficient stability for teachers to be confident of their practice in this area. The most telling information that teachers can draw on to make judgements about the effectiveness of their preparation of pupils, comes annually – the results. This infrequent feedback is perhaps not conducive to promoting reflection which augments practice. The learning environment constructed in Year 6 was closely linked to the pressures which the teachers indicated that they felt because of the tests. Additionally, only three of the teachers felt that other teachers in KS 2 (not in Year 6) were affected by test pressures. They thus seemed to feel that they were carrying the whole process, and its consequences, themselves. There seemed to be some sense in which Year 6 teachers were beginning to create a culture of competition. The perceived need to raise the ST score each year set each teacher against his/her own past performance. Furthermore, with each school aiming to raise its position in the league tables, Year 6 teachers seemed to set against each other. For one school to rise, another must fall.

The teachers were asked to identify the importance of different types of skills which the pupils might need in order to demonstrate success in the tests. Teachers' perceptions of the skills required in STs would no doubt have some impact on the methods and focus of pupil preparation for them. Figure 4.3 illustrates the skills which teachers identified as important for test success.

The teachers had particular views of the tests which showed clear distinctions between the different curriculum subjects. The very high factual recall nature of science tests was apparent. This was supported by the view that making connections in thinking were not

Very important .... of little importance

		1	2	3	4	5
Recall facts						
	Mathematics	4	7			
	English	2	3	5	1	
	Science	10	1			
Working at speed						
	Mathematics	5	5	1		
	English	8	3			
	Science	2	7	1	1	
Application to new contexts						
	Mathematics	8	3			
	English	5	5	1		
	Science	4	6	1		
Demonstrating learned procedures						
	Mathematics	8	3			
	English	4	4	2	1	
	Science	5	3	2	1	
Making connections in thinking						
	Mathematics	7	4			
	English	6	3	2		
	Science	4	7			
Understanding the questions						
	Mathematics	11				
	English	11				
	Science	11				
Other please specify	no responses					

Figure 4.3 Important skills for test success.

the highest priority. The task of demonstrating learned procedures was not regarded as a priority in English or science by a quarter of the teachers. The reasons were probably varied – in science because the knowledge was based on factual recall and in English because it was not thought to be based heavily on knowledge but – presumably be more creative. When the teachers were asked to indicate how they focused their ST preparation, the frequency and duration of lesson forms were identified as shown in Figure 4.4.

An attempt was made to establish the priorities teachers had in terms of the types of learning pupils required. It was assumed that there would be a link between the way pupils were prepared through lessons and the views and interpretation of the tests as perceived by each teacher. Teachers stated that little new information was taught during Year 6. There was a distinction between their teaching before and after Easter. After Easter teachers declared that there was virtually no new information taught, whereas before Easter there was some teaching of new information, mainly in maths and science, but very little in English.

Revision of facts to aid memory skills featured throughout the year. Four teachers claimed that between 11 and 15 hours a week were given to this type of teaching. This proved to be less of a feature in the teaching of English. Teachers claimed that near the beginning of the year they used lessons to try to highlight pupil misconceptions in English, mathematics and science. This featured as a major part of most core subject lessons. After Easter, this featured less prominently in the teaching.

Lessons that were designed for pupils to practise their learning by repeating skills and knowledge to develop improvement, featured most significantly before Easter. Teachers claimed that similar priority was given across the core subjects. After Easter, however, eight of the eleven teachers stated that they no longer focused on this type of preparation in English. There was a subtle difference in the priority given in English. This related to repetition, not in relation to improvement in types and forms of writing but in relation to speed in writing. Considerable emphasis was placed on speed practice in English, which drew a particular distinction with science and maths.

Lessons designed to encourage pupils to apply knowledge to new concepts seemed to be used by teachers across all three subjects in a similar way. Teachers claimed that there was a slightly greater emphasis on this after Easter, but they tried to ensure that it featured throughout the year.

Lesson types		none	<5	5–10	11–5	16–20	No response
Introducing new information	Maths (BE)	2	2	4	3		
	(AE)	3	5	2	1		
	English (BE)	2	5	3	1		
	(AE)	7	2	1	1		
	Science (BE)	2	2	4	3		
	(AE)	5	5	1	0		
Revising facts/ information aimed at helping pupils' memory skills for recall	Maths (BE)	1	3	3	4		
	(AE)	0	5	3	2	1	
	English (BE)	1	5	3	2	0	0
	(AE)	1	7	0	1	1	1
	Science (BE)	1	3	2	4	0	1
	(AE)	0	4	2	4	1	0
Assessment lessons to establish any misconceptions of problem areas in pupil learning	Maths (BE)	0	1	4	5		1
	(AE)	0	10	1	0		0
	English (BE)	0	3	4	4		
	(AE)		11				
	Science (BE)	0	2	5	4		
	(AE)	1	10	0	0		
Practice lessons – pupils to repeat their skills for improvement	Maths (BE)	1	6	2	2		
	(AE)	0	9	0	2		
	English (BE)	1	6	2	2		0
	(AE)	7	1	2	0		1
	Science (BE)	1	7	1	2		
	(AE)	1	8	0	2		
Application lessons – pupils apply knowledge to new contexts	Maths (BE)	1	6	4	0		
	(AE)	0	8	1	2		
	English (BE)	1	6	4	0		
	(AE)	3	4	1	2		1
	Science (BE)	1	7	3	0		
	(AE)	1	7	1	2		
Lessons designed to encourage pupils to reflect on their learning processes in order to evaluate their thinking (metacognition)	Maths (BE)	0	6	3	2		
	(AE)	0	11	0	0		
	English (BE)	0	6	4	1		0
	(AE)	1	7	0	0		3
	Science (BE)	0	7	2	2		0
	(AE)	1	8	0	0		2
Lessons designed to help make new connections between existing knowledge, e.g. Concept mapping	Maths (BE)	1	8	2			
	(AE)	3	7	1			
	English (BE)	1	9	1			0
	(AE)	4	6	0			1
	Science (BE)	1	8	2			
	(AE)	1	8	0			

(BE) Before Easter (AE) After Easter up until STs

Figure 4.4 Time spent on different aspects of test preparation per week.

Lessons that focused on encouraging pupils to make connections in their learning were emphasised more before Easter. They seemed to be linked to some extent with the teachers' aims to revise facts and information for memory recall. However, there seemed to be a less clearly defined view of the extent to which this could be developed, and most teachers indicated that less than five hours a week specifically developed these areas across the curriculum.

All the teachers were asked to indicate whether they designed lessons which were significantly intended to encourage pupils to reflect on their own learning processes (metacognition). All but one of the teachers claimed that they used this teaching approach. They claimed that it was used more before Easter. Five of these teachers stated that it featured in lessons which spent over five hours teaching per week in each subject.

The ways in which teachers were able to combine and develop these different types of teaching was not easy to explore in the preliminary group focus. The views and distinctions presented formed only an initial insight into some of the practices and priorities which were featuring in Year 6. What proved interesting to examine was the way in which the teachers made judgements about the 1998 test papers after their preparation and after presenting their views and details of teaching in the focus group. The teachers were asked to rank the key skills they felt were involved in the 1998 STs in each subject paper. In each paper they had to rank the different types of skills/knowledge between 1 (most important) and 6 (least important). Each of the 6 numbers had to be used with none repeated. The responses are summarised in Figure 4.5.

The results given presented an eclectic array of responses. On only a few occasions do more than half of the teachers agree with the type of learning required in the tests. The areas which seem to approach consensus relate to the importance of recalling facts in science (very important) and in English (least important). Working at speed seemed to be considered of little importance in mathematics and in science. Understanding the meanings of questions was considered very important in English by over half of the teachers, but not in the other two subjects. Some clustering can be seen in the views of teachers in the areas of making connections in thinking and understanding the meanings of questions in maths where these tended to be considered more important rather than less important. Demonstrating learned procedures seemed to be considered midway on the scale by most teachers. The area of applying knowledge to new contexts seemed to receive the greatest variance in response.

Knowledge/Skills	Example – Test paper	Maths papers 1	2	3	4	5	6	English papers 1	2	3	4	5	6	Science papers 1	2	3	4	5	6	No response
Recalling facts	6 (least important)	2	0	3	1	5	0	0	0	0	0	2	8	6	1	1	1	1	1	1
Working at speed	4	0	0	0	1	2	7	2	1	4	1	1	1	0	2	0	0	0	8	1
Applying knowledge to new contexts	1 (most important)	1	3	1	4	1	0	1	2	4	0	2	1	1	3	0	0	4	2	1
Demonstrating learned procedures	3	3	0	5	1	0	1	1	2	0	6	1	0	0	1	3	5	1	0	1
Making connections in thinking	5	1	4	1	2	0	0	0	3	2	1	3	0	0	2	2	2	4	0	1
Understanding the meanings of questions	2	3	4	1	2	0	0	6	2	0	2	0	0	3	1	4	2	0	0	1

Figure 4.5 Teachers' perceptions of the skills required for the 1998 Key Stage 2 Standard Tests.

Teaching strategies for preparing pupils for end of Key Stage 2 national tests

The teaching and learning that will have taken place throughout the period of schooling before Year 6 is clearly of significant importance. What is suggested here is that a period of preparation prior to end of Key Stage 2 tests is potentially a valuable time for a more focused type of learning which may promote a greater depth of understanding and interconnectivity. For a full range of learning to take place in the ways indicated, the central concern is for pupils to relate new knowledge to existing knowledge. This provides a challenge for all teachers at all key stages. If a teacher outlines information to which a pupil can make no links with his/her own previous knowledge then new learning will not take place in any meaningful way. This will result in two parallel knowledge systems – the teacher's and the pupil's. Pupils usually recognise the 'importance' of the teacher's knowledge and try to remember something of it. It is unlikely, however, that this will be put to much use on future occasions. To develop pupils' learning, teaching must help pupils relate new or recent information to previous knowledge in ways which enable them to process, structure and restructure it so that it can be used, applied and understood in a range of appropriate contexts. Changes in Year 6 teaching which, according to most QCA evaluation reports is occurring in almost all Year 6 classes, deserves careful examination and a theoretical basis which is educationally rather than politically grounded.

The challenges which teachers face when considering ST revision are summarised below under two themes – standards and accountability; learning.

Standards and accountability

- To prepare and equip pupils so that they have the best opportunity to achieve the highest scores possible.
- To learn from previous teaching, learning and assessment experiences so that schools can endeavour to demonstrate improvement from the previous year.

Learning

- Use the period of revision to promote greater understanding and interconnectivity of knowledge.

- To help pupils relate new or recent knowledge to previous knowledge in ways which enable them to process, structure and restructure it.
- To help pupils revisit areas of learning as individuals who are conceptually different and allow them to reconsider and restructure their learning.
- To create revision as an essential period of learning rather than a deviation from or interruption to teaching and learning.

Conclusion

Having identified that the end of Key Stage 2 tests call for pupils to demonstrate a range of problem-solving skills, some memorisation and a range of levels of understanding, preparing pupils adequately to tackle the content of them should not be regarded as a deviation from purposeful teaching and learning. (Developing specific test-taking skills is not included and requires a different type of preparation which is not the subject of the focus here.) A period of test preparation, in which pupils are given a range of learning opportunities, should not be seen as beneficial merely because of the implications of improved test results but for the development of learning being advanced. The opportunity to revisit areas of the Key Stage 2 programmes of study allows pupils to reconsider curriculum areas as individuals who are conceptually different from when these areas of knowledge were first visited. In order to learn successfully, it is important that pupils are able to link their knowledge – making new connections with existing knowledge, practise using and applying it in different contexts so that they can restructure and organise their knowledge, and reflect on the process of their learning. In order to help pupils learn in these ways, Year 6 teachers might consider the following five different lesson contexts as part of their planning and teaching in a period of test preparation.

Reminder opportunities – lessons in which key concepts are revisited so that any difficulties can be identified and clarified.

Repetition opportunities – in which pupils are able to repeat similar tasks – practice tasks – to use concepts, knowledge or skills so that learning can be more easily and quickly completed.

Recontextualising opportunities – these are to encourage pupils to practise their learning in new contexts.

Reconceptualising opportunities – in which pupils should be encouraged actively to seek links between different types of knowledge so that a range of possible connections can be considered. Concept mapping can be useful here, so too can emphasising the process of problem solving through class/group discussion.

Reflection opportunities – encouraging pupils to think about the processes used in learning in order to evaluate learning. These need to be structured by the teacher so that pupils are guided towards evaluating their learning – both motivationally and tactically. Practices associated with pupil self-assessment may be useful in this context (see Chapters 5 and 6 as well as Dann 1996a, b).

These five suggested aims for teachers are not intended to be seen individually but as a range of interconnecting opportunities, which together, will foster complex interactions to promote learning. Furthermore, pupils undertaking national tests need to demonstrate their knowledge individually. It is, therefore, important that pupils are able to do this. Accordingly, learning in the classroom should be internalised so that individuals have their own understanding of it. However, in the processes outlined above there is recognition of the social context of learning. As Bruner (1986: 127) contends: 'It is not just that the child must make his own knowledge his own, but that he must make it his own in a community of those who share his sense of belonging to a culture.' Thus, opportunities for social discourse should be promoted in the classroom. The balance between social learning and individual demonstration of it, in the model outlined here, need not be in conflict. Elliott (1998), as earlier discussed, highlighted as one of three points of great concern, related to what he regards as an objectives model of the National Curriculum and its assessment, that it focused on individual rather than social achievement. If, however, the process of learning undertaken within the National Curriculum can recognise and promote the importance of social learning – in Edwards and Mercer's (1987) terms – 'principled' learning which promotes shared understandings as well as individual demonstration of that learning as an outcome measure, the curriculum may not be distorted in the way Elliott presents. Surely, the measurable outcomes of the objectives model, that is the Standard Tests, do not necessarily have to adversely influence the whole of the learning process in schools even in the critical year when testing occurs. Indeed teachers are in a powerful position here to try to ensure that this is not the case. Their actions of mediation can turn the processes of test revision into valuable learning experiences. Without the tests, which have slowed down what Dadds (1999) has called 'the hurry along curriculum', developing and sustaining the five learning opportunities which have been advanced here may not be possible. Thus, the pressure, demands and expectations of the STs have most certainly created a curriculum pause. With strategic planning and deliberate mediating actions an assessment context can also become a powerful learning context.

Chapter 5

Pupil self-assessment: a case study

Introduction

Although part of the aim of this book is to consider some of the foundations of assessment and to construct a particular view of the relationship between learning and assessment there is an equivalent attempt to apply this thinking to classroom realities. With the focus in this chapter on self-assessment the way in which assessment can be regarded as learning is more strongly emphasised. The area of self-assessment is one which is often promoted but little understood. This chapter offers some theoretical grounding to support its possible role, function and impact in the classroom. Case study evidence to suggest its value and ideas for future development is presented. Relevant issues, more focused theory and suggestions for future development are continued in Chapter 6.

Issues and concepts broached in the literature are explored with particular references to their performance and priority. This chapter attempts to extend the conceptual framework already developed in previous chapters. In addition, it explores insights offered by a case study, however limited. A case study is outlined to illustrate the development and implementation of self-assessment in one primary school. The chapter concludes with a synthesis of the key issues relevant to self-assessment, and offers a range of strategies which may help further developments in this area.

The notion of self-assessment is not new. It has featured prominently in the development of Records of Achievement, particularly in secondary education. 'Self-assessment has beneficial effects on pupils' awareness, motivation and involvement in their work' (DES, 1989: para 4.9). Early National Curriculum documents indicated its potential:

Self-assessment by pupils themselves, even at the primary stage, has a part to play by encouraging a clear understanding of what is expected of them, motivation to reach it, a sense of pride in positive achievements, and a realistic appraisal of weaknesses that need to be tackled. It should be given due weight as part of the evidence towards teachers' internal assessments.

(DES 1988c: para 7.19)

Furthermore, space for self-assessment has featured on reporting and recording forms such as the Primary Language Record (ILEA, 1989) or whole recording strategies may be devoted to pupil self-assessment (Conner, 1991; Dann, 1996a). These and other references offer good intentions and a variety of ideas, yet they offer little to ground self-assessment into a rational theoretical framework or into coherent evidence based practice.

Theoretical starting points

Building on the constructivist perspectives developed in Chapter 2, the importance of pupils having an active role in the assessment process is an essential progression from pupils being active participants in the learning processes. The view that assessment and learning are necessarily interrelated gives a different emphasis and reciprocity to both. Assessment, in terms of judging the importance and priority of concepts, ideas and facts, and linking them to what is new is part of the learning process. However, the extent to which pupils engage in this process in a way which they can consciously articulate is a more complex issue. Nevertheless, the enormity of this challenge should not deflect intentions to further explore and develop insights into such processes. A fundamental premise which is sustained throughout this chapter is that self-assessment is part of the process of learning rather than just being one way of measuring it. Sadler (1989) has also argued this case. What is crucial here, therefore, is not the outcome of self-assessment but the process of self-assessment. This distinction begins to identify one of the most difficult aspects of self-assessment. Is it intended to serve the teacher as part of the information gathered on pupil learning, whether formatively or summatively, or is it to enhance pupil understanding of their own learning which may also help the development of metacognitive skills? In responding that it may well serve both, we are compelled to recognise the complexity of the emerging picture. The case study developed in this chapter is based mainly on the premise that self-assessment will offer useful information to the teacher whereas the discussion in Chapter 6 seeks to explore how self-assessment both draws on and develops pupils' learning.

Most attempts to develop self-assessment strategies have been concerned to invite pupils to articulate, whether through words (spoken or written) or through pictures, the assessment judgements they have made. Partly this may be in an attempt to provide evidence for the ways in which pupils have tackled the task. Additionally, it is designed to inform the teacher (or others) as part of formative or summative assessment processes. However helpful and even innovative, this intention is not without problems. In particular, it is essential to consider the rights of teachers and others in roles of educational power, to demand or expect the pupil to reveal his/her feelings and reflections on learning. Hartley (1997: 116–18) links this with Foucoult's notion of the 'confessional'. The possibility that more direct involvement of pupils in processes of self-assessment may only serve to increase and deepen forms of surveillance is thus raised. Once pupils have offered their own ideas and assessments about their learning they often lose control of them. Issues related to both production and control thus loom large in processes of self-assessment. Such notions have mainly remained as implicit within assessment literature to date.

In addition, but not entirely separate, there are issues connected with powers and responsibilities which are shared with pupils. Further discussion and analysis of these issues will feature later in the chapter in the case study context. At this point, the extent to which a development such as self-assessment provides an opportunity to share responsibilities and to communicate collaboratively within the classroom, must also be seen from the perspective of the pupils. What are their powers and responsibilities in the education system? What does the law, including documents such as the Children Act and the Laws on Human Rights, present and what do children perceive may also be at issue? What we might expect from children with regard to their engagement with the curriculum, and their responses within assessment contexts, be they formal or informal, may infringe on pupils' human rights. The intention to involve pupils in self-assessments, which might give the opportunity to extend the form and nature of assessment, assumes that pupils will wish to and be able to respond to such requests. Their right to contribute to the process of assessment may be as strong as their right to remain silent. The ways in which pupils respond to and develop their role in self-assessment will vary according to a variety of factors. Some illumination of these is evident in the case study, as well as in the further discussion in Chapter 6.

A case study on the introduction and implementation of pupil self-assessment in a primary class

The case study work carried out in Forest Grove Primary School was based on the school's interests and initial developments in self-assessment. The school was eager to work with researchers to further develop ideas and to review practice. The accounts given illustrate the practices developed. The role of researchers was participative in this school, working with the teachers, developing and piloting ideas (see Dann 1991 for full details). The self-assessment ideas are not intended to offer models of good practice. They were very much part of the school's own development process. Analysis of key issues, teased out from this case study, are offered later in the chapter. Here, there is some attempt to consider effective strategies and issues for self-assessment which are further developed in Chapter 6.

School context

The school involved was a small Church of England Aided Primary School. The catchment area was described by the head teacher as a social mix varying from 'Upper middle class, to people employed on the land, or, indeed unemployed'. Since the school was small (approximately eighty pupils) it occasionally worked as whole school. Additionally teachers often exchanged classes for single subject teaching. Assessment had been identified as an area for development and initiative (by the school rather than by any external measure). The head teacher regarded assessment as being intimately linked to a child's learning progress. In an interview, she saw it as a process of 'finding out where children are, which must be in relation to where they've been, so that you can place them in relation to where they are going'.

The school had developed an Internal Review procedure in order to handle pupils with behaviour problems. A simple record was designed to ensure that both parents and the pupil were involved in considering the problems and strategies for improvement. It was the development and use of this form of report and review that had prompted the staff to consider other ways of involving pupils in their own assessment.

The concept of pupil self-assessment in the school

The head teacher was committed to involving children in assessment:

> I think it's important for them to assess themselves, because if they don't know where they are, and where they are going, there's not much likelihood of them reaching or achieving their potential. It seems to me better if a child can learn to grow with himself rather than having someone poking and prodding (refers to the administration of standard tests).
>
> (Head teacher interview)

The process was very much concerned with involving the children in dialogue about their work and progress. The head teacher was very concerned that assessment should steer away from being a pencil and paper gathering exercise, divorced from helping the children about their work and how they can progress. She was keen for the pupils to be actively involved in setting 'mini-targets' which focused on one possible step forward in the learning process.

A parent governor who came in to the school during one of the visits expressed her opinion that pupils should be given 'space to express themselves'. She seemed pleased with the self-assessment initiatives at the school which she felt provided a good opportunity for the pupils to gain independence and responsibility in their own learning. She thought it important that teachers were willing to listen to pupils.

The school had previously operated a number of self-assessment initiatives from which new developments were to be a natural step. These ideas had been implemented by the head teacher while she had been teaching the Year 5 and 6 class. An art and design self-assessment had been implemented. Pupils were required to grade their enjoyment of the task from A to E and to indicate the level of their perceived achievement from 1 to 5. The criteria shown in Figure 5.1 were given to the children to help them make their judgements.

Pupils had to discuss their grades and levels with the teacher who would also indicate what she thought of the work through dialogue.

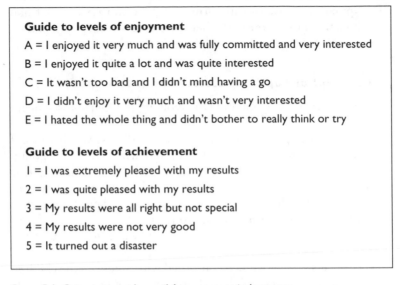

Guide to levels of enjoyment

A = I enjoyed it very much and was fully committed and very interested

B = I enjoyed it quite a lot and was quite interested

C = It wasn't too bad and I didn't mind having a go

D = I didn't enjoy it very much and wasn't very interested

E = I hated the whole thing and didn't bother to really think or try

Guide to levels of achievement

1 = I was extremely pleased with my results

2 = I was quite pleased with my results

3 = My results were all right but not special

4 = My results were not very good

5 = It turned out a disaster

Figure 5.1 Criteria to guide pupils' assessment judgements.

The head teacher had claimed that she had been pleased with this initiative and that pupils had responded sensibly.

Additionally, the school had tried 'Critical Partner Work'. Pupils had to read aloud their work while a partner listened. Following this they were both to answer a series of questions which sought to make them think about the quality of their work. The pupil guidance was given in the way shown in Figure 5.2.

The critical partner work had been developed to a second stage which was designed to focus more specifically on errors before redrafting work. The intention was for the children to learn to work collaboratively, cooperatively, and how to give and receive constructive criticism. The aims were very much related to pupils' learning rather than to gaining objective assessments. Stage 2 is shown in Figure 5.3.

The head teacher had encouraged the children to assess themselves in other aspects of classroom life. She had designed a wall chart which listed a series of questions related to personal behaviour such as: 'Have I been polite today? Have I been cruel? Have I been responsible? Have I used my initiative? Pupils were asked to think of their answers to these questions. Sometimes the head would discuss the issues with individual pupils.

Critical partner work
Stage I

Work with a partner . . .

Your task:
Read your work out loud.

Partner's task:
Listen carefully to your partner.

Both of you:
Try to answer the following questions:

- Do you think the writing is interesting and enjoyable?
- Is there anything missing in the piece of writing?
- Is there anything which is unclear or inaccurate?
- Can you suggest any helpful words or expressions?
- Can you suggest a more suitable beginning or ending?
- Do you think it is too long or too short?
- Could anything be missed out without spoiling it?
- Has the writer done what he or she set out to do?

Both of you:
Write down in rough any suggested improvements so that they can be thought about.

Figure 5.2 Critical partner work – Stage 1.

The head teacher was certain that these ideas had a positive effect on the children by motivating them and encouraging them to take responsibilities in their learning. She was keen to stress that the whole ethos of the school was intended to support the children in similar ways. Something of how this worked was observed on arrival in the school one morning. At the end of morning assembly the school secretary (also a qualified gymnastics coach) and the head

---

Critical partner work
Stage 2

Work with a partner . . .

Both of you:
Read through your writing again.

Try to answer these questions:

- Are there any spelling mistakes?
- Underline them with a pencil.
- Check the punctuation.
- Mark any corrections in pencil.
- Consider the suggestions for improvement, which you made in rough.
- Decide if you want to change anything.
- Show on your writing where you want to make alterations, if you do!
- Ask the teacher if you think you need more help.

Write out in best your revised version.

Figure 5.3 Critical partner work – Stage 2.

teacher asked all the gymnasts to stay behind in the hall. This included mainly children in the 'top' class who were also involved in the self-assessment work. The school gymnastics team was to compete in the annual county schools competition at the end of the week. The previous year there had been perceived discrepancies in the judging and many adjudications were considered unfair. This had resulted in many schools boycotting the competition this year. The school secretary had just discovered that apart from their school, only one other school was competing. Since the standard of the school's gymnastics was extremely high it was highly likely that they would win the competition but not really have any sense of challenge. Was it right that they should still enter the competition? This dilemma was presented to the pupils for them to consider. There were fifteen children in the group. All seemed keen to participate, offering the following comments: 'We've put in a lot of practice already'; 'We don't mind having just one other school'; 'Unless we work hard, they might beat us'; 'We don't know that we'll definitely win'. When put to the vote, all were in favour of participating. This conveyed a very inclusive approach to decision making in this example. It showed something of the school's philosophy in action.

All the developments already tried formed a starting point for new initiatives. The first part of their next initiative related to pupil self-assessment of research skills and attitudes. It was very much a summative approach, focusing on the topic work which had just been completed. The head teacher and class teacher of Year 5/6 had worked on the structure of the new self-assessment idea. They were beginning to feel slightly troubled about their work in self-assessment since the increasing emphasis on National Curriculum levels and standards seemed far removed from their work. They were keen to receive some evaluative feedback in order for them to decide whether or not to continue with their ideas. The pupil sheet in Figure 5.4 had been devised by the head teacher and class teacher.

The class teacher reminded the children about some of the lessons they had covered in the topic. The children were asked to say what they could remember. Her promptings were mainly in relation to curriculum areas. The children then contributed a range of different themes in each subject related to their topic on water. The class teacher explained the self-assessment sheet – part A only first. All but one (Peter) of the children were listening. This particular child was hurriedly colouring E's on the assessment wheel in Section B. For Section A the pupils were asked to discuss what they thought with a partner. They all had their topic books available. Most of the pupils seemed to be talking to each other about what they enjoyed. There was little evidence of pupils selecting the same 'favourite' part of the topic. Question 2, however, had been more problematic. Many of the pupils had identified items of knowledge which they thought would be useful at a future date – such as that nine-tenths of an iceberg lies below the surface of the water. Some of the children had highlighted skills which they felt were useful – such as how to draw maps, how to set up an experiment and lay out a letter. Question 3 invited mixed responses. Some claimed that they had no areas of difficulty. Others identified an aspect which they found hard but often could not say why. Those who did offer a reason usually referred to the fact that they found it difficult because the experience or knowledge was new. There was no attempt to think about and articulate the concepts involved.

Critical self-appraisal of research skills and attitudes
To be completed at the end of a period of work on a topic.

Name _____ Age _____ Date _____

Section A (to be completed by pupil)
1. Which parts of the topic have you most enjoyed?

2. What skills (not facts) have you learnt?

3. Did you find any of the work difficult? If so, try to say why

Section B (to be completed by the pupil and teacher together)
A is the highest grade and E the lowest.

Key to qualities
1. Attitude towards class work
2. Out-of-school research
3. Cooperation with a group
4. Ability to study alone
5. Ability to use reference skills
    (Did you know where to
    look for material?)
6. Ability to select relevant
    material.
    (Did you manage to find out
    exactly
    what you wanted from the
    material?)
7. Attitudes towards solving
    problems
8. Final presentation of
    information

Section C (to be completed by pupil and teacher following discussion – pto.)
Action which needs to be taken as a result of this profile: a small step forward.

Figure 5.4 Critical self-appraisal of research skills and attitudes.

After a short break the children settled to consider Section B. All but one (Peter, again – still colouring in E's) were listening. Each of the eight qualities were discussed in the lesson so that pupils would be sure what they meant. Most of the pupils seemed confident in tackling the task. One pupil (Sandra), however, with special needs, needed to have one-to-one interaction with an adult in order to attempt this task. Any engagement with this self-assessment process in the way promoted here assumed a certain degree of ability and awareness. In Sandra's case the potential to participate was evident but not in its presented written form. Selecting appropriate strategies which are inclusive for all pupils thus requires careful consideration.

Section C required discussion with the class teacher. There was insufficient time to complete this process during the session. Those children who identified a mini-target managed this in a variety of ways. Some children found it hard to identify something which would be relevant in a future topic and promoted a target which was related to learning a specific fact. In discussion with the teacher these targets were modified in order to be meaningful in a new topic context. Trying to understand who 'owned' the targets, which were more heavily steered by the teacher, remained a question at this stage.

Significant issues

Several aspects of this pilot summative self-assessment were problematic. First, the self-assessment initiative seemed to be a bolt-on to the topic. The problems encountered with children not being sure of the difference between facts and skills might well have been alleviated during lessons as the focus of a lesson was explained to pupils. Second, the use of a grading system of A to E was developed by the head teacher and class teacher. Although ways of interpreting these grades within the given task were offered, it is not clear how the children used them. (This is further discussed later in the chapter.) Additionally, the mini targets which were agreed between the pupil and teacher were not clearly considered in the light of how they might be used in the future in terms of a focus for learning. Some of the limitations which the initiative highlighted related to its emphasis on summative assessment. In discussion with the head teacher and class teacher, the idea of developing a formative self-assessment process was promoted. The head and class teacher were keen to do this in language since they had already developed the critical partner work. By the next visit to the school the head and class teacher had developed another self-assessment format – Critical Self-Assessment in Language (CSAIL). The ownership was very much school based. However, the head teacher and class teacher wanted the researchers to help implement this by working with a small group of children (half the class, all Year 5) to develop the initiative with the children and to evaluate it. This marked a very distinctive shift from the teachers' undertaking action research, which was facilitated by discussion and interaction with researchers, to the researchers becoming 'action research agents' (Dann 1991). Methodologically, this is a significant re-emphasis, which seemed to result from the sudden uncertainty teachers felt in developing creative and innovative ideas within an increasingly prescriptive National Curriculum framework. (This work was preliteracy hour but within the framework of the National Curriculum English requirements.)

As a pilot initiative in developing self-assessment there were issues requiring consideration relating to the role of the researchers in the classroom. Understanding pupils' perceptions of the researchers would be critical in analysing the pupils' contributions in feedback, in discussion and in negotiation. Furthermore, collaboration between the researchers and the class teacher would shape the nature of the way in which the self-assessment would form part of ongoing formative assessment. (Both researchers had spent a significant amount of time in the classroom before the CSAIL pilot work.) Additionally, the researchers needed to gain some insights into the way the pupils worked and the standards which could be reasonably expected from them. It was recognised, however, that the researchers were in no way as informed about pupils learning as a class teacher would be. In discussion with the head teacher and class teacher about the impact and nature of the proposed pilot it was decided that using researchers might encourage the pupils to be more honest about their work and feel in a stronger negotiating role when they saw that the researchers were slightly more distant from immediate classroom issues and consequences. Some of the issues related to the research structure are explored in discussion later in the chapter.

Initially there were fourteen pupils in the pilot group (an additional Year 5 pupil joined the school part way through and was also included). The class teacher described most of the group as 'fairly bright'. One pupil (Jason) had particular problems with writing and was receiving extra help each morning with this. A second pupil (Tristan) had been identified for internal review because of his behaviour problems.

Critical self-assessment in language
To be completed (a) with a partner; (b) with a teacher; (c) both following discussion

Name _____ Age _____ Date _____

Grades A = very good B = good C = reasonable D = not very good E = need much help	Grade given by self	Grade given by partner	Final grades agreed with teacher
Spoken language Ability to tell a story or short piece of news in detail with accuracy and vividness			
Ability to give a short illustrated talk 'live': think of preparation, presentation and audience reaction			
Drama – mime			
Drama – acting			
Listening Ability to concentrate and listen to a long, unfamiliar story with no pictures and then show understanding of it			
Ability to receive and give complicated messages and instructions			
Writing Factual accounts or report (Think about what you believe makes it interesting)			
Imaginative stories (Think about what you believe makes it interesting)			
Poetry			
Ability to draft and rewrite			
Handwriting			
Reading Can you say which kind of reading material you like most?			

THE WAY AHEAD
(Only one area may need to be highlighted)

Speaking

Listening

Drama

Handwriting

Personal Writing

Reading

Signed _____ (pupil)

_____ (teacher)

Figure 5.5 Critical self-assessment in language.

Each weekly visit to the school would focus on one area of the CSAIL. One researcher took the role of 'teacher' throughout and the other as observer and evaluator. Not all parts of language would be involved in the pilot but a selection would form a sample for review and evaluation so that future developments could be considered.

The first week focused on listening skills. The children were told that they would be doing something like the 'research skills self-assessment' (carried out a few weeks before) during this lesson. It was indicated that their own views of what they had learnt were important and would be part of this lesson. The lesson began with class discussion of why listening was important and in what contexts it was useful. Three short passages were read to the children. After the first two there was whole class discussion about what these passages were about. Following the third passage (from *The Empire of the Sun*) children were placed in pairs to ask each other questions about what they had read. The idea was for them to give both themselves and their partners a grade (A to E), as used on the previous self-assessment activity. Most of the children engaged in this purposively except for two, one of whom would not answer any questions (Jason) and the other (Emily) was very negative, saying that it was too hard. Soon after the task had been implemented it was clear that the idea of the pupils formulating their own questions to one another and basing assessment on the answers given, was not the best approach for many of the children. The questions which the pupils formulated were obviously a product of their own understanding. This had not been accounted for in the assessment process. The decision to exclude assessment of the questions and to promote collaboration leading to peer assessment in this first activity was unwise. It revealed that we had insufficient knowledge of the children's abilities in language to differentiate the work appropriately and that the skills being demanded were not yet developed in many of the children. The children responded in the lesson saying that they found using the grades difficult – 'I'm not sure how to choose one'.

In the interviews with all the children involved at the end of the pilot work, several of the children mentioned that they did not enjoy this session. The two children who were clearly not engaging with it at the time, raised this lesson, unprompted. Emily said that the stories were 'boring' whilst Jason commented that *'Empire of the Sun* was hard to listen to because I did not understand it. I preferred it on the telly'. In reviewing this session, it was recognised that listening skills were particularly difficult to assess and were perhaps not the best choice. Whereas it was thought that this would not provide any written obstacles for children, in fact it had presented a different set of problems. The way in which children were to select grades was evidently something which they were unsure about and needed to be addressed in a different way in subsequent sessions. This uncertainty featured despite children's previous experience of similar approaches to self-assessment. The developmental nature of children's learning in this area started to become apparent. Before continuing with other sessions a structure for the lessons was devised which would try to blend the teaching of the curriculum in language with teaching for the task of self-assessment. A structure was devised which was carried through for the rest of the sessions.

1   The task was introduced – for example – writing poetry, writing factual accounts of an incident, handwriting . . . (all related to the CSAIL sheet).
2   Time was spent talking to the pupils about the particular task: what was it? . . . Why do we do it?
3   Pupils were asked to say what they thought would make a good piece of work in the particular area outlined.
4   From the pupils' contributions and the 'teacher's' (researcher's) own expectations several criteria were written down on a large piece of paper which would be left out on the table during each session. For example, for poetry lesson the pupils were to consider: whether the poem was based on an interesting idea; whether it made you think; whether you wanted to hear it again; whether it flowed well. For writing an imaginative story the agreed criteria were – having a good introduction, describing the characters, having a snappy title and a good ending. Care was taken not to be too prescriptive. The use of language was recognised as being a complex and creative process. There was no desire to tram-line the pupils' thinking but to broaden it.
5   Having outlined criteria which would be used to help them both undertake the task and to assess it, it was necessary to try to ensure that the pupils could translate the criteria into practical application. A number of examples of possible 'products' of the task were shared with the pupils for them to consider – to identify the strengths and weaknesses and to offer reasons for the thinking behind these judgements. This was considered an

important step in helping the children understand what they were aiming to achieve in the lesson.

6   Since the model of assessment, which had been devised in the school to be used for self-assessment, was based on the use of grades some consideration was needed in helping the children relate the grades to the criteria for the lesson. Thus, in using examples to exemplify the criteria (point 5 above) grades were also awarded so that pupils might gain greater understanding of how the grades were intended to indicate the extent to which the criteria had been fulfilled.

7   The various speeds at which pupils worked in completing the task called for some requirement for some of them to redraft, add illustrations or elaborate their work in some way.

8   Half-way through the term, it was decided that when the work was completed, but before the self-assessment, pupils should all be reminded of the task criteria. This additional element of the structure was based on the judgements made in the early observations, when the grades awarded and the reasoning given were not always clearly associated.

9   Pupils worked in pairs on their self-assessment. They had different partners for most of the sessions who, on all but one occasion, were selected for them (based on the recommendation of the class teacher).

10 The pupils were to allocate a grade to themselves then, having read their partner's work, give their partner a grade accompanied by an explanation for why the grade had been allocated. Both grades were recorded on the CSAIL sheet.

11 A third grade was then recorded which resulted from a discussion between the pupil and the teacher.

12 Each pupil was invited to identify one aspect of his/her work which might form the focus for the remainder of the term.

The ways in which the pupils participated in these processes and issues related to its development are discussed in the following seven sections.

Assessment 'versus' the curriculum

This initiative seemed to be specifically assessment-led. It was aimed at extending one particular aspect of assessment practice in the school. However, it was intended to serve both teaching and learning.

In isolating one aspect of assessment there was an obvious danger of losing sight of the breadth and interrelationship that needs to be incorporated into school-based assessment practices. The children were very aware that these lessons were linked to self-assessment. Furthermore, they were working with two 'outsiders', which might have given a message that assessment was divorced from normal classroom practice. Additionally, there was a danger that the assessment practices might overshadow the curriculum in a way that was not intended. At the end of the pilot work, as part of the individual pupil interviews, all the children were asked a deliberately unspecific question at the start of the interview: 'What do you think about the things that you have been doing in our group? Approximately two-thirds of the pupils referred to the language (curriculum) aspects of the work, rather than the self-assessment. Of the five children remaining three gave very vague answers from which it was difficult to ascertain what they had conceptualised as the focus of what they had been doing, and two specifically mentioned the assessment work:

> It's a good idea. There is a certain way to go about it and it should not be done in one go.
>
> (Keith)

> Quite good, when I go to secondary school, then get a job it will be good to talk to people about work.
>
> (Clive)

From this question it seemed that most of the children had separated the assessment and curriculum components and emphasised the latter. However, it may be that in mentioning curriculum details they were implicitly referring to the self-assessment which accompanied them.

In trying to explore in more detail how the pupils made sense of the self-assessment they were asked whether or not it had helped them think about their work in a different way, as well as any areas in which they felt they now needed to improve. Only two of the fifteen children stated that the self-assessment had not really helped them: 'I don't really think about it, I just get on with the work' (Jeremy). All the other children indicated that it had helped. Two of these children were unable (or unwilling) to explain why. Three considered its value in subject specific terms, two referred to the criteria outlined, upon which the subject tasks were based. A number of other comments paid general attention to processes of reasoning and the development of meaning behind the acquisition of self-assessment skills:

> It helps you make up your mind about what it really means. You get to know what to say and what it really means.
>
> (Asif)

> They've made me think about the reason for a grade.
>
> (Roy)

Such skills were not easy and many of the pupils had mentioned that they found the self-assessment difficult at the start. Furthermore, one pupil stated that: 'If you don't concentrate it won't be good' (Anna), which emphasised the commitment required for self-assessment in order for it to be of value. Another pupil stated the benefits of the self-assessment on her work in terms of: 'When I take work home I spend more time on it' (Emily). After a deliberate pause, aimed at drawing out an explanation, she said: 'Because you can see what it is for' (Emily). It seemed that the self-assessment had provided some additional framework of purpose for learning activities which had somehow added a new dimension to her attitude towards work.

This was further illustrated by Jason, who commented that: 'They've given me some good grades which made me feel that I'm improving according to my difficulties'.

Although Jason refers to the grades which he received, rather than those given to himself, he had evidently internalised them in a way which had changed his attitude to his work and achievements (the impact for Jason is further expanded in relation to the role of criteria later in the chapter.)

When the children were asked to indicate whether the self-assessment had helped them see how parts of their work could be improved, the majority of pupils highlighted an aspect of language work which they now felt able to improve. Two of the pupils (Tristan and George) stated that the self-assessment work had not helped them identify positive ways of improving their work. Although pupils were positive about the potential to help improvement, most were not able to give specific details and offered comments such as: 'Yes, with poetry', or 'Yes, it has helped me'. It may well be that improvements lie more in the domain of attitudes and approaches to work rather than with specific content improvements.

The pupils were asked whether the self-assessment had helped them to realise aspects of their work in which they were good but which they had not previously recognised. All but three of the children indicated that they had gained some further insight into their work through looking at specific task related criteria. These seemed to have encouraged the pupils to realise that their work often fulfilled the requirements of these criteria, whereas previously their achievements may have been masked or overshadowed by other, more embracing non-specific criteria. Two of the three who had responded negatively stated nothing more than 'No', whereas the third presented more of an indifferent stance: 'Sometimes I'm good, other times I'm not, it depends if I want to' (Jeremy). This echoes Anna's previous comment regarding the level of commitment given to the work, which, in this instance is not necessarily maintained at a constant level.

It seemed that the relationship between the curriculum and self-assessment was a complex one which did not permit the two to be easily separated. The teaching style adopted had been one which it was hoped would particularly draw together these two components in a way which gave specific attention to the role of the pupil. Thus, from the pupils' comments, it seemed that they indicated that the process of teaching which led to their involvement in assessing their work was an integral part of the whole process. One of the key ways in which the teaching and the assessment were to be linked was through the use of the same criteria for the tasks as for the assessment. The ways in which the pupils understood the nature, scope and role of the criteria is explored in the next section.

The nature, scope and role of criteria

One of the main difficulties in developing criteria related to trying to ensure that they were neither too vague nor conversely, too specific. Specifying criteria appropriately is daunting for any involved in the process, yet the task seems to be compounded when the criteria are to be used and understood by pupils.

The strategy adopted in the self-assessment initiative focused on illuminating collaboratively with the pupils a few criteria for each task. These, when taken in isolation were fairly general. However, they were further clarified and discussed in relation to particular examples and interpretations which could be developed in the specific language work in the session. The importance of translating criteria into actual examples was considered to be a useful means of helping to reduce the degree of abstraction which is required in grasping criteria. Such a step was considered to be beneficial when dealing with young children whose conceptual understanding may be limited. Thus for example, in considering the writing of a report, the importance of a short snappy title, an introduction stating what and where the report is about, including plenty of detail, descriptions of the characters involved, and a clear account of what happened were all highlighted and discussed.

The emphasis on trying to ensure that pupils grasped the nature of the task was vital for their role in assessment. The teacher's approach in seeking to develop a shared understanding of the elements of the task rather than imposing a strategy was considered important. However, the pupils' responses to this approach varied.

In the pupil interviews an attempt was made to establish what governed their thinking while assessing their own and a partner's work. When asked to say some of the things which they thought about whilst assessing their work, two-thirds of them mentioned criteria such as 'neat writing', 'funny bits', 'whether it's messy', 'number of full stops', 'how it looked on paper' 'whether they spoke up', 'whether I took my time', 'writing and imagination', 'whether it makes sense'. All these had featured in some way as criteria for different tasks. However, there was no way in which it could be proved that these were combined with other shared criteria and changed from task to task. What the comments do show is that the pupils were able to use criteria, even if only partially to inform their thinking about their work.

Two of the children were explicit in talking about the list of criteria used in each lesson. They indicated how these were important for judging their work. However, the reasons they gave were very different. Keith stated: 'Because we write to please them, because we know what they want. The effort we put into it is not so important.' George remarked that the criteria: 'Told us what to look for which was helpful.'

Keith seemed to indicate that the stated criteria should be taken on board and accepted despite personal preferences which may differ. He seemed to allude to the fact that the criteria were imposed, dictating the work required. This, he considered, did not necessarily reflect his perceptions of effort or achievement. The criteria almost seemed to him to be a contrivance for conformity which were not negotiated and which quashed his own views and perceptions.

George, on the other hand, approached the criteria in a different way. Even though there was some sense in which he saw the criteria as imposed (indicated by the word 'told'), he used them to help understand the task. He seemed to indicate that the criteria were integrated into his learning and understanding which helped him make sense of the tasks and their assessments.

An interesting individual case was noted which further illustrates the role and function of using criteria. This involved Jason, who had particular difficulties with handwriting and was receiving special help for this for a short time for three mornings per week. It seemed that the difficulties which he had with writing overshadowed the rest of his work and he seemed to be very dismissive of most of the work that he did, even if it did not contain much writing. His response to the first CSAIL session, which focused on listening, was indicative of this since he refused to answer any questions saying that it was too difficult for him. It was during the second CSAIL session that the role and use of the criteria seemed particularly helpful to Jason. Having written his poem (which visually seemed extremely messy) he was very disappointed with it. He gave it a D grade saying: 'Its no good, it's a mess'. His partner had awarded a B saying 'I liked it; it made me laugh'. The poem was read to the whole group (along with others). Comments from the whole group were: 'It's brilliant', 'It's funny', 'Can we hear it again?' They decided that it was worth an A grade, which left Jason speechless. In filling in the agreed grade with the teacher, Jason was asked what he thought about the grade he had been given by the group. He said he was pleased because: 'My writing didn't matter'.

This incident seemed particularly significant in indicating a role which the criteria played. They focused on a limited number of skills so that 'everything' was not important all of the time. In Jason's case his writing difficulties had pervaded all his work and it seemed that the attempt to focus on just a few criteria which, in this case, did not include writing, had actually allowed him to see that he could achieve something and that his work was not as bad as he had originally thought. Jason had mentioned this achievement in poetry during his interview highlighting that it had helped him to feel more positive about his work.

The second incident occurred towards the end of the term and related to the writing of factual accounts and reporting. Jason was writing a report on a school trip. As he was writing he seemed pleased with the quantity of work produced and with his handwriting. On several occasions he had nudged the person next to him to show how much he had written. (If asked to grade his work at that point one might speculate that he should have given himself an A.) His success on this particular day with handwriting was, however, not an item which would be specifically included in the assessment, which to Jason was obviously not a welcomed decision. When it came to the self-assessment, he suddenly seemed to realise that, in relation to the criteria, his work was not as good as he had thought. In response to the need to give a self-assessment, he shifted drastically to the other end of the scale and awarded himself an E saying that his report was 'boring'. His partner, however, considered his work more favourably and awarded a C which showed an interesting attempt to bring his work into line with the criteria. This seemed to boost Jason's confidence once again and to give him an added sense of achievement since he had both made a good attempt at the task and also made headway in his writing which obviously continued to be important to him.

This incident showed a different role which the criteria played from that in the first example. In this case the criteria initially detracted from Jason's concern to improve his handwriting and failed to give specific credit for it when there was marked improvement. However, once he had discussed the work with his partner and received his grade, as well as talking to the teacher he seemed able to see success in both his task and writing skills. This example showed that the pupils were not necessarily totally concerned with the criteria outlined. In this case, because of Jason's specific difficulties, he had been encouraged to articulate 'other' factors which he thought were influential to his work. It emerged, however, that most of the pupils, in thinking about their pieces of work, considered additional criteria to those outlined.

Twelve of the fifteen pupils claimed in their interviews that in assessing their work they considered either or both of the following: their performance in relation to their previous work; and/or the amount of effort they had put into the task. There was no scope given to the pupils to address these explicitly in assessing their work. All of the criteria were related to specific aspects of language and not to self-referenced perspectives. It was evident from the pupil responses at interview that they perceived developments in their work in relation to past performance and to the amount of effort put into tasks. Trying to push these issues to one side had not been achieved. The awarded grades were masking the reasoning behind them. By not asking the children to include such issues had not meant that they were unconsidered. It was clear that many of the children were aware of the extent to which self-referenced judgements influenced their thinking and commented on them. Three further examples are given.

When grading the task of giving an 'illustrated talk', Asif had awarded himself D/E while his partner had offered a grade B saying: 'It was good but could have done with a bit more preparation because he read a bit of it from a list which was boring'. Asif said: 'I can do much better than that; I hadn't tried as hard as I could.' Thus, although his talk was good he felt that it was considerably below his own expectations. (The agreed grade was B.)

The second example concerns the session on poetry writing. Sheema had awarded herself a B for her poem and her partner had given an A. Sheema said she liked it, and it had taken her all afternoon to write. When it was read to the whole group they thought it was: 'a bit dull', 'boring', 'alright', 'quite ordinary really'. They decided it merited a C grade. Sheema did not seem very pleased with this decision, although she did say that it was not 'very' good. At interview Sheema commented that she felt that grade C for her poetry was 'unfair'. It seemed that her effort was significant for her and was not recognised. In both these examples the agreed grade reflected the criteria for the task and did not formally acknowledge the pupil's other concerns.

The third example, however, noted an exceptional response. It concerned Jason and the session on handwriting. Jason had awarded himself grade A for his handwriting explaining that: 'This is the best I've ever done'. His partner, however, had offered grade D saying apologetically. 'It looked a bit of a mess really'. If taking the criteria alone, D would seem a fairly generous grade. However, in reaching an agreed grade with the teacher, on this occasion Jason's self-assessment was supported. The decision here was based on the overall aim of the self-assessment idea: to facilitate pupil learning. In this particular case it would most probably have been counterproductive to have stuck too rigidly to the specific criteria and thus fail to deliberately acknowledge the obvious improvement in work for which he had particular special needs and required encouragement. The self-assessment was not required for external accountability and thus the requirement to adhere to the criteria was not absolute. Rather, the priority given to pupil learning required a large degree of sensitivity in balancing the promotion of specific criteria with personal and individual factors. This highlights a necessary emphasis on the role of pupil self-assessment in a formative context.

In exploring the pupils' understanding and use of criteria further, the pupils were asked what they considered when assessing a partner's work. Half of the pupils mentioned particular criteria such as 'length', 'interest', 'neatness' or stated more generally that they looked for the things which they had discussed at the beginning of each session. Of the remainder, most referred to whether they liked their partner's work or not, or how it compared with their own attempt. This proved to be an interesting discovery since it revealed that the pupils were keen to adopt other criteria in assessing their partner's work as well as their own. The 'other' criteria seemed to consist of comparing their partner's work with their own in order to give a grade. Obviously it was more difficult for the pupils to relate their fellow pupil's work to their previous work since they had insufficient knowledge. There was one exception which related to how others in the group assessed Jason's work. One of the children pointed out: 'You would treat it differently'. Some attempt was being made here to make allowances for his specific difficulties even though these were not requested.

One comment illustrated the pressure which pupils felt to reciprocate with a high grade if one had been received. 'If they gave you an A you feel that you ought to give them a good mark' (Jeremy). It seemed interesting that this had not featured more prominently in the pupils' responses. From observing their attempts at peer assessment there seemed to be no further evidence to support the idea that pupils felt obliged to give certain grades. It must be noted, however, that the pupils had been specifically paired for the peer assessments so that they were not with close friends.

It seemed that it was only Jason who expressed particular difficulties in relating the criteria to someone else's work in order to make an assessment. He found assessing another person's work difficult: 'Most people are better than me so I don't know what it is like'. In observing Jason in his 'assessor' role he did not seem to struggle. It may well have been that he allocated grades based on how he expected others to perform rather than on the work presented. If a person has little knowledge or understanding of the achievements conveyed in another's piece of work, the extent to which it can be assessed is surely limited. It seemed clear that Jason was able to ascertain that other work contained things which his did not. The impact of such discoveries are not insignificant. There seemed to be a great many issues which loom large when peer partners are at very different levels. The particular case of Jason as part of the group offers some insights here.

Issues concerning grading

The discussion concerning the role and function of criteria has already briefly referred to aspects of the grading of their work in relation to self-assessment, peer assessment and grade negotiation. Furthermore, the general procedure outlined for each session involved translating criteria into grades. It quickly became apparent after two sessions that the pupils found it difficult linking the criteria to the grades. The reasons for this are no doubt complex but seemed compounded by the time lag between when they discussed the grades (beginning of the lesson) and when they were applied (at the end of the lesson). Introducing an additional step in the lesson structure to remind the pupils of the links between the criteria and the grades was thus initiated. They seemed to be particularly useful for pupils to develop their thinking and skills in this way at the start of a new development.

Although it was intended that the pupils should be guided towards grading in relation to the agreed criteria, as already indicated in the interviews, they often considered other factors than the stated criteria when allocating a grade. Such considerations could not be eliminated or suppressed if they were meaningful to the pupils. Yet the structure of the system did not specifically account for such thinking. The self-assessment was intended to help the pupil understand their learning so that future steps could be more easily identified and moved towards. However, the head teacher and the class teacher were keen to develop a system which might have some clear structures and criteria. From observing the ways in which the pupils repeatedly made sense of the criteria in their own ways, and combined them with issues and considerations that were important to them, the grading system seemed to have limited use. It did not allow a stan-dardised used of the criteria nor did it reveal the basis of pupils' own judgements. During each CSAIL lesson the pupils would have three grades – his/her own self-assessment, a peer assessment and an agreed grade with the teacher. From the interviews with the pupil it seemed that it may well be that the basis for these grades might all be different. There was no attempt to record the rationale for the grades, since it was assumed that meanings were shared. Without a more detailed level of understanding, the self-assessments were not fully formative. It may have been of greater value not to include the grades. The grades were an additional layer of abstraction within the process with a role and function which seemed dubious. Using the criteria alone, with scope for pupils' own additional criteria, may have been preferable. However, it should also be recognised that the pupils tended to see some sort of status in using a grading system, which would be lost if it were dropped. As a new initiative, the pupils seemed to identify grades with importance and status. By being asked to offer grades they perceived that they were sharing in something of importance and of high status. Such perceptions would be closely linked to existing practices and priorities at both a school and national level. If the pupils were dealing only with criteria there may be a diminished sense of importance and status. It might be over hasty to give undue significance to the complex interaction between assessment, the curriculum and pupils' learning experiences, particularly in the early stages of a new initiative when pupils' previous experiences and interpretations needed to be considered and prioritised.

The process of negotiation

The self-assessment procedure adopted was one which was designed to include an 'agreed grade' made with the teacher after the self and peer assessments had been given. This was intended to provide an opportunity for pupils to talk about their grades and discuss their own perceptions of their work with the teacher. It also provided the teacher with an opportunity to offer his/her assessment of the work and give a rationale behind the judgement in relation to the criteria for the task. Any discrepancy between teachers' and pupils' grades could then be discussed so that an agreed grade could be recorded. The process of negotiation experienced in the pilot work was not, however, as intended. This became evident in several ways which are considered below.

The timing of the negotiation within the group sessions was not favourable. Obviously, it needed to be towards the end of the session in order to draw on all the relevant factors to be considered. The pressure of time in each session often resulted in there being very little time left when the children had finished the task. Also, children who managed to finish their work well within the time were able to engage in the process of discussion with the teacher more fully than those who worked at a slower pace.

The majority of the grade agreements were undertaken when the group was reassembled at the end of the session following the self and peer assessments. Those who had finished in good time would have already discussed an agreed grade with the teacher. For most of the children there was little scope for discussion and exchange since time was short. Each pupil would articulate the two grades already given (self and peer assessment); the teacher would respond with a grade which seemed to best fit the stated criteria with a brief reason for this judgement. The 'agreed grade' was therefore rather more of an imposed one by the teacher with little encouragement given to involve the pupils in discussion and agreement through the process of negotiation.

As far as the teacher was concerned this aspect of the assessment work was problematic as it did not develop in the way intended. Since the whole initiative was new and developmental it was felt that the negotiation aspect of the work was not the key priority and could be further developed and refined subsequently. The need to prioritise aspects of the self-assessment process had not really been considered. The aim had been to introduce the whole initiative and to regard the whole process as developmental. The limitations and difficulties in applying the 'negotiated' grading aspect highlighted the differences and complexities of the initiative as a whole. Furthermore, it indicated that greater attention needed to be given to the development of individual aspects of the self-assessment rather than the promotion of the whole initiative.

From the interviews with the pupils, something of their reactions to and understanding of the grade agreement was explored. The children were asked whether they thought that the agreed grade was 'fair' and whether or not they wanted to disagree with the agreed grade but thought that they should not challenge it. Eleven of the fifteen pupils stated that they thought that the agreed grade and accompanying teacher explanation was 'fair'. One pupil stated:

> With some people they give you anything . . . Oh she's a goody goody. But he (teacher) gives you what your work is worth whether he likes you or not.
>
> (Asif)

Another pupil commented that the giving of an agreed grade by the project teacher (not their normal class teacher) was not easy: 'It's difficult because he's not used to us since he does not know what we are like' (Sheema). This may have given the pupils an added sense of authority since they may have felt more confident about their own grades than those given by someone who was unfamiliar with their work. Conversely, however, there may have been a sense in which the whole process could have been seen to be undermined by a feeling that the project teacher was not sufficiently knowledgeable about the pupils to comment adequately on their work. There seemed to be little evidence to support this view since the majority of pupils claimed that they were generally content with the proceedings. The possible impact of pupils being overcautious with their answers, so that they respond in the way which they perceive to be most acceptable, cannot be overlooked here.

The way in which a teacher handled the process of negotiation was seen to be a crucial factor in the future development of the self-assessment. Some pupils were not entirely happy with the grades they received, not, it seems, because they did not trust the teachers' judgements of their work, but because they had different opinions based on their own criteria.

Two of the pupils said that they thought that the grade agreement was only 'sometimes' fair. One expressed a particular instance when he had awarded himself a B but the agreed grade was C, which he seemed to dislike. The other pupils wondered about the reasons underlying her receiving a higher 'agreed' grade than her self-given grade. Her sense seemed to be of wonder rather than injustice. Both, however, said that they would not disagree with the teacher even though they thought that their grades should be different.

Another two of the pupils said that the agreed grades were not fair. One of these (Tristan) gave a specific example where the two grades, given by himself and a partner were A and B but the agreed grade given was D. Although at the time he agreed that this work was not fulfilling the stated criteria, he claimed that 'I still think I should have had more'. This pupil showed no indication of wanting to disagree directly with the teacher over the given grade. It would, therefore, seem that although he felt that in his opinion his work deserved a higher grade he did not feel able to negotiate his point with the teacher. The other pupil (Keith) exclaimed that:

He (project teacher) grades according to your partner's grade, but says yours is the most important. If he likes you he gives you better grades.

Keith had previously commented on the importance of the criteria in influencing his own assessments. His view here implied that it was the teacher who was not using the criteria appropriately. This was the only pupil who commented that he felt that he wanted to disagree with the 'agreed' grade rather than accept it blindly. However, he did not feel that he should actually say anything to the teacher. He said that on one occasion he felt that the teacher's grade did not sufficiently account for his imagination and he felt that the grade should have been higher. This challenge indicated some resentment of the fact that he was not given unlimited freedom to judge his work. This particular pupil had revealed his dissatisfaction with the testing practices in the 'normal' classroom routine and seemed to want to fully seize the possibility of making assessment meaningful. He was evidently disappointed with the parameters in which he was to work which were more restrictive than he hoped.

Although the majority of the pupils indicated that the agreed grade was not in fact a negotiated grade but a teacher given grade, even if they felt that it was unfair they did not see their role as being in any way part of discussing any discrepancies. The agreed grade procedure tended to be a swift affair which the pupils saw as having over-ruling powers which could supersede their own grades.

The process of 'negotiation' seemed to be a sensitive and problematic area. It was a process which needed to develop and it required a nurturing of trust and openness between the pupils and teacher. For the teacher, it seemed that the danger of dominating the procedure needed to be positively recognised and actively remedied. However, some acknowledgement that the negotiation process required some sort of leadership and could not be equally shared between teacher and pupil, was needed. The teacher, as the organiser of appropriate learning materials and a pupil's guide through the pathway of learning, must remain as the senior partner. As part of the self-assessment scheme, it seemed that negotiation potentially offered an important channel through which the whole meaning and significance of the assessment could be communicated. Yet its initial promotion was not without difficulties. The use of a grading system in this initiative may have further contributed to some of the difficulties encountered. Only an agreed grade was recorded, which if different from the other grades (self and peer) was not accompanied with a reason or justification. Thus, to see a different (lower) grade recorded could appear undermining. Having a written explanatory comment regarding the agreed judgement made would have been more helpful.

The scope of a process of negotiation must be related to the purpose of the self-assessment being promoted. For a scheme that is intended to be formative in purpose the use of grading in the process of negotiation seemed unhelpful. To agree comments which relate to completed work seems to be a more appropriate basis for negotiation. This may allow a greater sense of collaboration rather than overruling. The extent to which a more reciprocal process of negotiation involving an exchange of judgements and interpretations could be developed requires further research and development.

Identification of mini-targets and their possible subsequent value in learning

One of the most important features of the self-assessment initiative, which the head teacher had illuminated, was the opportunity for pupils to identify an aspect of their work to which they could pay special attention for improvement. It was intended that their targets should be stated for each aspect of the language work. Only one or two targets were anticipated so that the prospect of endeavouring to attain them did not appear too burdensome. The formulation of mini-targets, as with the process of negotiation, seemed to play a different role in the implementation of the self-assessment scheme compared with the planned intentions. Mini-targets were to be elicited following the grading of work. Once identified, emphasis was to be placed on ensuring that pupils were aware of possible ways of achieving these target areas. This was something to which the teacher needed to contribute a little guidance.

During the pilot proceedings a negligible amount of time had been spent on the formulation of mini-targets. Most of the pupils had at least one comment recorded on the back of their sheets, but no attempt had been made to explore possible avenues through which improvement might be achieved. The unusual situation of having a different teacher for this initiative offered an additional obstacle to developing strategies for following up the targets within the full classroom context. Liaison and discussion with the class teacher about mini-targets was not carried out on a detailed basis until the end of the term. Both the head teacher and the class teacher were keen that the pupils should be aware of a mini-target, and that they be supported to achieve it. However, translating this intention into classroom realities was more problematic during the initial phase of self-assessment. As with the agreed grades, there was an intention that negotiation should feature as the process through which a mini-target was agreed. In reality, however, the mini-targets were mainly those indicated by the teacher. Comments such as: 'I don't think we need to write down a mini-target – do you?' and 'I think we can put something on the back which you can think about – what shall we put?' were frequent. Although both these teacher comments asked for a pupil response the teacher's view was already clearly stated, so leaving a rather restricted and channelled scope for pupil contributions.

The pupil interviews provided an opportunity to try to establish what pupils had understood and remembered about their mini-targets. Three of the pupils had no targets recorded. Only one pupil from the whole group was able to recall the mini-targets recorded on the sheet. Four pupils, when specifically asked, said that they were unable to indicate any areas which they thought they would like to improve. However, two of these children had indicated elsewhere in the interview that there were aspects of their work which they would now need to further develop. It therefore seems that failure to identify mini-targets did not necessarily mean that they did not appreciate points for improvement.

Most of the pupils identified areas of work for improvement which were not those written on their sheets. These tended to be quite focused points which related to a specific piece of work, and had featured in discussions surrounding their work in the sessions. For the mini-targets to be of use and relevance in future learning, the pupils needed to be able to understand them in ways that could be related to new learning experiences. Accordingly, they needed to move beyond the specific task criteria. The level of thinking and understanding required here was not explored in this initiative; the formation of mini-targets was assumed to be fairly unproblematic. Strategies to further consider and develop this aspect of the work are studied in Chapter 6.

The role of the peer partner

The grading of a pupil's work by a partner was an integral part of the assessment scheme being developed. Its aim was to encourage pupils to articulate reasons behind the grades given, and for them to have the opportunity to consider work other than their own. The development of peer assessment was seen to be a supporting component of promoting self-assessment. The requirements of the peer partner were kept fairly uniform throughout the development of the initiative. After the first session, however, the need to consider carefully the role and scope of the peer partner's task was highlighted. During the 'listening skills' task the pupils were required to ask each other questions in order to establish the extent to which they had understood the passage that had been read to them. This method required the pupil to formulate his/her own questions, which were obviously within the limits of their own understanding. The partner's performance was, therefore, confined within the limitations of his/her own understanding. To some extent this is necessarily the case with peer assessment. However, when work is presented in a more direct form, a peer can still recognise aspects of work which are different and beyond their own.

The case study revealed some indications that pupils were not always rational in allocating grades. Anna claimed after one session involving peer assessment: 'I'm not always in the mood'. This showed that results were sometimes unpredictable and pupils' willingness to sustain commitment to their work was not always complete. However, from the data collected, inconsistencies related to their possible immaturity seemed minimal.

It seemed that the grading of a partner's work, compared with grading their own work, drew on different information. Both should have been centred around the criteria outlined for each task. However, as indicated when pupils were marking their own work they considered factors such as the effort which had been put in and the standard of work in relation to his/her own previous performance. When marking a partner's work (given that peers did not select their own peer partners) they were usually unable to draw on personal factors related to their partner (except in the case of Jason's work upon which pupils specifically commented). Thus, when considering a possible grade to allocate, pupils could work with the criteria given, make comparisons between their own work and their partner's work or try to include a judgement related to perceived expectations of their partner based on their knowledge of their partner's general classroom practice. A complex combination of these seems likely. The research, however, did not probe this area more deeply. In trying to encourage pupils to consider criteria more specifically, it may be that looking at someone else's work enables more objective judgements to be made than in cases of self-assessment. Certainly it encourages another way of under-standing learning.

The self-assessment initiative highlighted potential obstacles to peer assessment. Anna had indicated in her interview that she found some people's work hard to read (meaning decipher). To overcome this, in some of the sessions, a sample of pupils' written work was read to the whole group. This offered an alternative way of accessing other pupils' work, and attempted to overcome the possible limitations of written formats limiting thinking about achievements.

Relating self-assessment to other classroom assessment practices

An important part of the pupil interviews was to try to establish something of the pupils' reactions to, and perceptions of, their previous assessment experiences. The class teacher had explained that she had tried to encourage self-assessment with this year group before the new self-assessments. This had been carried out through pupils marking their own and each other's work. Additionally, she claimed she tried to ensure that she made time to talk frequently to the pupils about their work and their marks. She pointed out that this was not yet part of a specific assessment plan but the start of developing practice.

The pupil interviews were designed to probe the pupils' under-standing and interpretation of the classroom assessments, which they had already experienced. When the pupils were asked if they had ever been given the opportunity to mark their own work, eight of the fifteen said 'no'. The remainder mentioned occasions when they marked each other's work or checked in the answer book. Those who failed to identify any of these self-assessment opportunities had not been able to recognise these classroom events as involving them in the assessment process.

In addition to exploring their regard for any self-assessment carried out before the new initiative, pupils' responses to the marking they received were considered. Five of them stated, unquestioningly, that the class teacher's marking was as they expected it to be; neither too high nor too low. The ten pupils remaining, however, highlighted various concerns that they had with regard to marks being either too high or too low. Five of these were linked to specific incidents or areas of the curriculum, whereas the remaining pupils expressed a more general view of the marking as being either too generous or too hard. However, there was a strong sense of 'but she knows best' (Tristan). Such a belief seemed to be reinforced by the pupils' perceptions of their role in talking about their grades with the teacher. Only three of the pupils claimed that they had ever discussed their grades with the teacher. This seemed to be an unusual response, since the class teacher had mentioned how she endeavoured to ensure that they all had an opportunity to talk to her about some of their marks during the term. It may well have been that the informality and spontaneity of such encounters almost went unnoticed by the pupils. On the contrary, it may have been that the class teacher had achieved less than she intended with the limited self-assessment which she had encouraged. A further consideration is related to the fact that any early self-assessment encounters with the class teachers would have been very different from the strategies and structures of the new self-assessment initiative. It may well have been that their inability to recognise such opportunities was more related to their now holding new ideas of what grade negotiation and talking about assessment was like.

Further exploration of classroom assessments focused on topic tests in order to compare and contrast the pupils' perceptions of this form of assessment with the self-assessment. The pupils were asked: if they ever had tests; (if yes) how/if they found out how they got on in them; whether they thought that tests were fair and why they thought they were given tests. All but one confirmed that they had regular spelling and mathematics tests and also an annual reading test, which had recently been completed. They explained that these were usually given in for marking and they later received the papers back with marks and comments. One of the pupils claimed that he never really found out how he got on with these tests and was not satisfied with receiving comments and a mark. He offered the following comment:

> As you go up through the years they (tests) get harder, but your scores stay the same even though you improve.
>
> (Keith)

There seemed to be a distinct dissatisfaction here with the way in which tests failed to reveal real improvements. This contrasted with the self-assessment initiative, which seemed to have sparked a great enthusiasm for this particular pupil. The rest of the pupils, however, seemed not to take strong objection to the use of tests or to any limitations in the information they conveyed. Of particular interest was the reasoning which the pupils articulated for being given tests. Only one of the responses indicated any sense in which the tests were intended to help them: 'They tell the teacher and us what we need to improve and have practice on' (George). The remaining comments were all concerned with tests being used by the teacher 'to see if you have learnt things' (Jackie), 'to see how good you are' (Tristan), 'to see what you've learnt' (Roy), 'to see if you have improved in school' (Keith), 'to see if we bother to learn' (Sally). They seemed to have a summative focus. These responses provided a marked contrast to the purposes which the pupils associated with the self-assessments which were linked to helping them to improve.

The children were asked why they thought they had been asked to try the self-assessment in the series of lessons which they had received. There was a strong sense in the responses that the pupils thought that the self-assessments were designed to be of help to them:

> 'It's to help you really' (Asif).

> 'To help you when you go to secondary school because teachers won't always be there to go up to' (Sheema).

> 'Now I'm better at it, and my work' (Emily).

> 'To make us look at our grades more and discover why teachers give us those grades' (Richard).

> 'To make us stop and think about what we do and if we can improve' (Sally).

> 'So we can learn how to do it; it will be useful in our jobs' (Clive).

> 'To make us understand things more and improve' (Anna).

> 'It's good to do; it will help us when we are older' (Jeremy).

These eight pupils all clearly indicated their perceived benefits of self-assessment, mainly in terms of being able to gain greater understanding of their own learning. The foresight which some of them displayed in trying to suggest its benefit for them in the future displayed a sense in which they were able to project the essence of the scheme from the immediate context to a different environment.

Not all the pupils, however, saw the self-assessment initiative to be wholly supportive. Two of the pupils (Keith and Jason) indicated that the scheme was designed to see whether they were able to cope with self-assessment so that the teachers could find out what they could do and 'next time we'll have harder sheets' (Jason). This almost hinted at a perceived conspiracy. Yet both of these pupils had revealed particular enthusiasm for the scheme and expressed the benefits, which they had gained from it. It seems that at this stage of the initiative, these pupils were not entirely sure of the motive for using the self-assessment process. This was further qualified by four more of the pupils who said that they were not really sure why they were doing this work and one more, who claimed, that its purpose was to make sure that 'we tell the truth to the teacher' (George). From looking at the full set of responses for all fifteen pupils, all indicated that aspects of the self-assessment had helped them improve their work. This contrasted with their view of classroom assessment, which associated less directly with promoting their learning, and more with enabling the teacher to check up on them.

Conclusion

The case study highlighted one school's attempt to further develop their assessment practices. The specific details of the structure and format of self-assessment are not offered in any way as an example of good practice to be repeated. Indeed they are born out of specific school circumstances and policy developments. What the case study does help to illustrate are significant issues related to assessment processes. Issues related to structure are explored in relation to the ways that they are interpreted by those involved. From such analysis some attempts to present principles for future development are offered in Chapter 6.

Ways in which pupils make sense of assessment (including self-assessment) are an important part of the research. Of significance here are interpretations of how pupils understand their learning and the way it develops. Some attempt to identify aspects of self-assessment which helped pupil understanding and those which were more of an obstacle or hindrance were explored. It was evident that factors introduced as part of self-assessment could not be assumed as unproblematic, easily conveyed and adopted by pupils. Pupils had particular and sometimes idiosyncratic views of what they were being asked to do. They were making complex judgements about their work and their learning which drew on a variety of factors and influences. Trying to ignore these would only serve in portraying a facade covering the realities of learning and assessment. Highlighting a potential role for self-assessment in the primary classroom, which is positively and enthusiastically received by pupils, is only a small step. In order to gain greater understanding of the ways in which pupils may engage with the role and responsibilities of participating in self-assessment, a more thorough investigation of the possible ways in which pupils are motivated and skilled to take on this role needs to be offered. In this light, self-assessment must be more firmly located within a framework of life-long learning which accounts for pupils' developing skills and motivation. In this vein the possibilities and practicalities for self-assessment, highlighted in this chapter, can be related to more rigorous and compelling arguments that are grounded in a broader theoretical framework related to both learning and assessment. Indeed, the theoretical framework that is elaborated in Chapter 6 seeks to locate self-assessment into a theory of learning that embraces assessment and thus promotes the notion of assessment *as* learning.

Building a framework for self-assessment

Introduction

Having briefly outlined some origins for pupil self-assessment and examined one primary school's attempt to develop a self-assessment initiative, this chapter builds on Chapter 5, aiming to focus more specifically on a framework for self-assessment as well as offering practical considerations for its future development. Of particular concern is the relationship and balance between assessment, which seeks to establish and measure pupil performance in relation to objective criteria, and assessment which directly seeks to influence and develop a pupil's sense of personal identity which includes his/her understanding of self as life-long learner and achiever.

In exploring the possible learning foundations for National Curriculum related assessments (Chapter 2) it seemed that the pupils' role in the assessment process was active in terms of their capacity as test takers or curriculum participants, but passive in the sense of their being directly influenced by the processes or outcomes of assessment. Increasingly, evidence suggests that pupils are far more greatly influenced by their experiences of assessment than is specifically recognised (Pollard *et al.* 2000). Even when the focus is on formative assessment, teachers tend to regard any impact on pupils mainly in terms of intervention and mediation. Torrance and Pryor (1998) offer a different view. They suggest that pupils need to make sense of assessment in order for their learning to advance. Pupils need to understand something of the gap between where they are in their learning and where they might be. Although the next step of learning may be teacher constructed or nationally prescribed, if it is not grasped by the pupil, as an aspiration, next step, target or goal, then it is unlikely to be realised. The advocation of teacher/pupil collaboration, to reflect Vygotsky's practice of constructing a zone of proximal development, offers a strategy for learning development within a constructivist framework (Chapter 2). However, if learning is viewed in this framework, the way in which assessment relates to this understanding needs more careful consideration. Torrance and Pryor (1998: 16) suggest that, to date, there is insufficient literature to indicate how teaching, learning and assessment interrelate within constructivism. With the emphasis on the individual pupil in an active role interpreting and constructing learning, there seems to be a need to appreciate that this active participation should also be recognised within assessment. This, of course, assumes that assessment is regarded in a formative sense, which will contribute to the development of learning.

Of further significance are the ways pupils perceive their academic abilities. These may partly be gained from their understanding of assessments made on them by teachers and others who contribute a view to their learning. Additionally, they will also be influenced through a variety of interactions and experiences. Nicholls (1984) clearly indicates that children's perceptions of their academic ability changes during their time at school. At entry to primary school pupils have a positive view of their own competence, sometimes with grandiose evaluations of their abilities (Benenson and Dweck 1986). By the time they leave the primary phase their self-perceptions of their competence is much lower. Paris and Byrnes (1989) consider possible reasons for this, one of which is that young children (up to ages 8–9) do not differentiate between academic and social academic abilities. There was little notion of academic achievement as separate from personal preferences and effort. Furthermore, children gained different insights into the criteria for assessment shifting from the belief that social praise and effort denoted achievement to a view that social comparisons and external evaluations were the key indicators of achievement. Accompanying this shift in understanding, some children became more negative about their achievements since they viewed the level of effort given to their work as no longer having the impact on achievement that they had previously believed. It certainly seems to be the case that as children pass through primary school their assessments are increasingly legitimated by external factors. Pupil experiences and perceptions may well reflect the views of Nicholls, and Benenson and Dweck (op. cit.), yet the process of self-assessment may offer a context and process for helping to shape and influence pupils' understanding of their developing achievement in a complementary way which can be initiated, developed and sustained throughout the process of life-long learning.

Establishing a purpose and need for pupil self-assessment, in an ideological sense, has important but only limited relevance. Translating the view that self-assessment is important, into practical possibilities is a more complex but crucial task. This chapter outlines and explores a number of processes, requiring development and understanding, before considering the details of how self-assessment might be utilised in classroom contexts. Of particular concern is the notion of self-regulation, which includes self-efficacy, motivation, metacognition, and feedback.

Self-regulated learning

If self-assessment is to be advanced, there is an implicit assumption that pupils are encouraged to participate in a process which will give them a greater stake in understanding and developing their learning. More than this, however, it can be seen as a process which relates to a broader view of pupils' learning development. In addition to the theories of Piaget and Vygotsky which contribute to a constructivist perspective, pupil understanding and interpretation of their learning is crucial rather than optional (Chapter 2), the notion of self-regulated learning requires some explanation.

The idea of self-regulation has its roots in the sphere of biology. Organisms respond to the environment through processes of biological feedback and adaptation. Its provenance in education is clear in Piaget's work, and since then has been applied to learning and development theories from varying perspectives. Fundamentally, self-regulation is 'an organising concept, self regulated learning describes how learners cognitively, motivationally and behaviourally promote their own academic achievement' (Zimmerman and Schunk 1989: ix). Pintrich (2000: 452–3) highlights the following four assumptions underlying models of self-regulation in a learning context:

1 The active, constructive assumption – implying that learners are viewed as active constructors in the learning process.
2 The potential for control assumption – that all learners can potentially control, monitor and regulate aspects of their own cognition, motivation and behaviour as well as some aspects of their environment.

3   Goal, criterion or standard assumption – to which comparisons can be made or decisions as to whether the process should continue or be changed can be made.
4   Mediation between personal and contextual characteristics and actual achievement or performance feature in most models of self-regulated learning. Thus, outcomes in learning will, to some degree be influenced by self-regulatory processes.

The capacity of learners to demonstrate and utilise these aspects of self-regulation, and the sophistication they bring to these skills will relate partly to their developmental growth. There may, as Zimmerman (1989) suggests, be limitations in the ways in which very young children are able to be self-regulating in their learning. Thus, their capacity to self-regulate needs to be considered less formally at this primary age. The reasons for pupils' more limited capacities vary according to cognitive and social perspectives. Piagetians would assume that the egocentric nature of young children would limit their capacity to self-regulate, whilst Vygotskians would emphasise young children's restrictive capacity to use language covertly to guide self-regulation. An additional perspective may highlight the limited development of the higher order thinking skill of metacognition in young children which needs to feature within self-regulation. However, even with limited yet developing capacities, it is suggested that pupils can still have a participative role in the process.

When pupils' cognitive skills are considered to be sufficiently developed, their use of self-regulation in learning might operate in the following ways (from Zimmerman 1989: 4):

• Personally improving their ability to learn through selective use of metacognitive and motivational strategies.
• Proactively selecting, structuring and even creating advantageous learning environments.
• Choosing the form and amount of instruction that they need.

These processes clearly outline the potential for pupils' self-regulated learning. However, personal, cultural, social and institutional factors present constant restraints. The extent to which pupils display and develop self-regulating functions within their learning, in a proactive sense, is partly based on their willingness to use such strategies. Constructivists would tend to claim that motivation for learning is intrinsic and that a distinction between motivation and learning is not helpful. Nevertheless, as the goals of learning become more explicit, formalised and part of national expectations, pupils seem likely to make more conscious judgements about their participation in this prescribed form of 'school' learning. Pupils will need to make a judgement about the extent to which they can operationalise self-regulatory processes in learning. Obviously this is unlikely to be in a calculated informed way, but as part of the process of under-standing the assumptions and dynamics of teacher/pupil interactions in the classroom.

Self-efficacy and motivation

The way in which a pupil enters into a teaching, learning and assess-ment interaction that serves to promote development will, to some extent, depend on each pupil's self-efficacy. That is, their personal belief 'about having the means to learn or perform effectively' (Zimmerman 2000: 17). Zimmerman also indicates that self-efficacy beliefs can causally influence a pupil's use of self-regulation in academic time management, academic learning strategies, resisting adverse peer pressure, self-monitoring, self-evaluation and goal setting. He illustrates with the example of goal setting. The more capable pupils believe themselves to be, the higher the goals they set for themselves. If pupils fall short of their goals, those who are self-efficacious will try to increase the efforts they make, whereas those who are not will tend to withdraw. A pupil's belief in his/her own potential achievement seems to have an impact on the way s/he seeks to bring this into effect.

Within a school learning context, however, teachers (rather than pupils) tend to structure and present learning goals. The expectation is that pupils are motivated and able to fulfil these goals. If they are not achieved, the evaluative and monitoring process in our current educational system is highly likely to point to poor teaching quality as the cause of poor pupil performance. Boekaerts and Niemivirta (2000: 418) present a more complex picture. They promote the notion of a 'learning episode' in which a person is

> invited, coached, or coaxed to display context specific, goal directed learning behaviour. If the learner accepts this invitation, his or her learning behaviour unfolds over time until one of the following conditions is met: (1) the learning goal that organised

the learning episode is attained, (2) the learning goal is attained only partially, but this state of affairs is accepted by the learner, (3) the learning goal is reappraised as unattainable, unattractive or irrelevant, or (4) another goal takes precedence.

The 'success' of the school-based, teacher-led learning episode is dependent on the way in which a pupil engages with the goals and purposes presented. Boekaerts and Niemivirta (2000) question the extent to which pupils create an experience of 'felt necessity' in the focus teacher-led learning. However, they suggest that children often construct highly sophisticated and progressive learning episodes in natural contexts where opportunity and 'felt necessity' coincide. They call for a recognition of pupils' own personal goals as significant influences in the learning process.

In addition to pupils' beliefs in self-efficacy is their motivation to be active in their learning. For pupils' learning to progress, there must be some self-motivation in order to take advantage of the learning environment of which they are a part. Obviously, pupils' beliefs that they can achieve will form part of their motivation. Other factors which may impact here are worth some consideration. The motivation to learn may be considered as an inherent part of development. Piaget, for example offers little suggestion that children may not be motivated to learn. Rather, the processes which drive the development of cognition are considered to be embedded in an individual's biology and his/her interaction with the environment. Such an explanation does not provide an adequate account of the realities of classroom learning in which some pupils are clearly not motivated to learn to the same extent as others. Rheinberg et al. (2000) suggest that motivation within learning relates to individual characteristics such as motives, interests, goals, beliefs as well as to situation related factors such as the nature of the task, potential gains or losses, characteristics of the environment. Children will make judgements about the extent to which they wish to engage with learning. These, Rheinberg (1989) (in Rheinberg et al. 2000: 511) suggests focus around the following four questions:

1   Does the outcome seem to be determined by the situation? If the answer is perceived to be 'yes' then the pupil is unlikely to be motivated; if it is 'no', then together with perceptions of other key issues a pupil may be motivated to learn.
2   Can my actions have sufficient impact on the outcome?

3   Are the potential consequences important enough to me?
4   Do the desired consequences follow from the outcome?

For questions 2, 3 and 4, if the answer is 'no' it is unlikely that there will be pupil action. Whereas, if the answer is 'yes' pupils are more likely to be motivated to endeavour to achieve. For those children who are not propelled to action based on factors of motivation, there may be issues of volition which need to be considered. Some individuals will exercise volitional control processes that enable them to overcome the adverse conditions which they identify. So, for example, pupils may try to control their attention, their emotions, the environment or their cognitive processes in ways which help them proceed with learning – as an act of will. Such acts of volition are not easy and are difficult to sustain.

Pupils' skills in self-regulated learning may be accomplished more fully in adolescence rather than in their primary years. Yet, the argument presented here calls for some sensitivity and recognition of aspects of development throughout formal schooling. Dewey (1963: 48–9) in discussing the purpose of education states that

> the most important attitude that can be formed is that of desire to go on learning . . . What avail is it to win prescribed amounts of information about geography and history, to win ability to read and write, if in the process the individual loses his own soul: loses his appreciation of things worthwhile, of the values to which these things are relative; if he loses desire to apply what is learnt and, above all, loses the ability to extract meaning from his future experiences as they occur?

The enthusiasm for learning which is so often present when a child begins primary school needs to be harnessed and utilised. All too often, as Covington (1998: 5) suggests, 'their enthusiasm, like that of previous generations, will also dwindle and soon evaporate'. Attempts to encourage and motivate pupils to learn and to have the belief in self-efficacy certainly should not be postponed to secondary education, where it may be too late. Developing strategies which are consciously designed to promote pupils' beliefs in their own potential to learn should be specifically embedded in the primary curriculum.

Bandura (1997) identifies four possible ways in which self-efficacy is learned and how this learning may be influenced and supported:

(a) performance accomplishments; (b) vicarious learning; (c) verbal persuasion; (d) physical/affective status.

(a) Performance accomplishments refer to the way a pupil's performance is received influencing self-efficacy expectations and actions. So, for example, poor grades and negative feedback have the potential to lower self-efficacy beliefs.
(b) Vicarious learning is undertaken by observing or interpreting the way other pupils behave and the work that they do. Pupils who make judgements on others and see their own progress and learning as limited in some way as part of this comparison are likely to have lower self-efficacy beliefs.
(c) Verbal persuasion – the messages that are conveyed to an individual from others will all contribute to the way an individual constructs his/her self-efficacy beliefs. Messages may be overt or covert, intentional or unintentional – it is the way that they are interpreted which will impact on self-efficacy beliefs.
(d) Physical/affective status – Environments in which there is conflict, tension, anxiety or uncertainty are unlikely to offer contexts that promote positive self-efficacy beliefs. Classroom pressures, resulting in pupil anxieties, may have a significant effect on developing pupil outcomes and beliefs.

Various strategies may be employed within the classroom to promote pupils' positive beliefs about learning. The potential role which self-assessment may have for helping pupils to consider their work honestly and positively, to express their own views about their learning, to engage in the process of celebrating achievement and to establish future priorities, seems to offer the potential to influence the process of self-efficacy as part of the process of self-regulation. Even if pupils have more negative views of their learning, self-assessment can be specifically focused so that positive aspects can be framed and crystallised. As in the example with Jason in the case study, this approach improved his view of what he could do.

Metacognition

Put simply, metacognition is thinking about thinking. Within self-regulation theory it is an essential component that enhances the mechanism through which feedback is acted upon and judgements are made. Similarly, the process of self-assessment demands that judgements are made by the pupil about his/her achievements. It requires thinking about learning. In terms of cognitive processes, metacognition is a higher order skill which develops throughout primary education. Beyond a basic and rather simplistic definition is twenty-five years of research, which has tried to offer more precise definitions. Hacker (1998: 11) seeks to draw together some consensus.

> A definition of metacognition should include at least these notions: knowledge of one's knowledge, processes and cognitive and affective states; and the ability to consciously and deliberately monitor and regulate one's knowledge, processes, and cognitive and affective states.

Two strands are implicit here: understanding knowledge; and recognising one's own role in monitoring and regulating it (an aspect of self-regulation). Both strands are required, for simply possessing knowledge about one's cognitive strengths or weaknesses alone does not indicate metacognition. It is the way that this knowledge is utilised in assessing the realisation of learning goals and targets which must be evident. There is a core assumption that some form of self-monitoring or assessment is required. Hacker (1998: 13) states that

> the key to effective self-regulation is accurate self-assessment of what is known or not known. Only when students know the state of their own knowledge can they effectively self-direct learning to the unknown.

With reference to cognitive monitoring, research has shown that even young primary aged pupils can accurately monitor their knowledge. With progressing age this capacity increased along with accuracy. For example, a study by Flavell *et al.* (1970) focused on children aged from 5 to 9 (in Hacker 1998). They were shown successively longer sequences of pictures of familiar objects. The children were than asked to predict whether they would be able to recall the pictures in the correct order. The children's predictions were compared with their actual recalls. The youngest children tended to overestimate their recall ability whereas the older children were able to recall more pictures and were more accurate with their predictions.

Studies which have sought to explore cognitive regulation have shown that 'young children can be trained to monitor their strategic behaviour and performance, and that this training can enhance their regulation of efficient strategies' (Hacker 1998: 17). Thus, children at a young age can make judgements about ways of working, and make appropriate decisions about relevant strategies. At the primary school age limited experience restricts the choices available. Nevertheless, the processes for cognitive regulation are evident and could be further enhanced by specific training and awareness.

Feedback

Within the context of self-regulation feedback is identified as a controlling factor (Carver and Scheier 2000). From a behavioural perspective, they highlighted four key elements which form a feedback loop: an input function; a reference value; a comparator and an output function. Black and Wiliam (1998: 48) highlighted elements of feedback drawn from the behavioural sciences which focus more specifically on possible elements of feedback. These include:

> data on the actual level of some measurable attribute;
>
> data on the reference level of that attribute;
>
> a mechanism for comparing the two levels, and generating information about the gap between the two levels;
>
> a mechanism by which the information can be used to alter the gap.

For a feedback loop to be completed there needs to be some altering of the gap between performance and the goal/standard or reference level. Without this, feedback has not taken place. Kluger and DeNisi (1996) identified different responses which may be selected in response to the gap identified as part of feedback:

- to attempt to close the gap and reach the standard;
- to abandon the standard completely thus eliminating the gap;
- to alter the standard so that the gap is not so great;
- to deny that a standard exists, which effectively removes the need for feedback.

In recognising that feedback responses vary considerably some attempt has been made in recent research to offer explanations for this. Black and Wiliam (1998) summarise some of this research. Attention is drawn to the evidence which suggests that individuals should be directed towards tasks rather than self for better performance. Feedback such as praise tends to emphasise self rather than task, and Black and Wiliam suggest that this has little impact on performance, although it can increase interest and attitude. An additional finding indicated that feedback on learning processes seems more effective than feedback on absolute levels of performance. Black and Wiliam (1998: 53) offer a definition which uses feedback in its restrictive sense as

> any information that is provided to the performer of any action about that performance. This need not necessarily be from an external source, nor need there necessarily be some reference standard against which the performance is measured, let alone some method of comparing the two.

However, in accord with Sadler (1989), for assessment to be formative, feedback is essential. Without it information is simply recorded and not acted upon – the control loop cannot be closed.

Torrance and Pryor (1998) suggest that feedback forms an essential function of formative assessment. Although it is clearly identified as the part of assessment which allows the judgements made to contribute towards future learning, it is problematic. Details of the interactive process of feedback are scarce in research literature. Furthermore, drawing from Sadler (1989) they reveal:

> The common but puzzling observation that even when teachers provide students with valid and reliable judgements about the quality of their work, improvement does not necessarily follow. Students often show little or no . . . development despite regular, accurate feedback.
>
> (Torrance and Pryor 1998: 13)

Hattie and Jaeger (1998) extend the notion of feedback more specifically to processes of learning. They move away from the more behaviourist assumptions underlying much of feedback analysis which emphasises input and output factors, including Black and Wiliam's similar emphasis on the provision of information, to the importance of pupils' *understanding* of information and learning. Their model is based on 'the tight interplay between assessment, learning and feedback' (p. 111). Their view of learning recognises that in order to assess learning and to improve it there needs to be an understanding of the 'constructions that students have made from the learned/taught information' (p. 113). As suggested in the discussion of constructivism earlier in this book, students will make sense of the information they are taught in different ways. In order for learning to advance, both the teacher and pupil must consider the process of learning as well as the outcomes. Feedback must be related to understanding and not merely to partial evidence which may measure only an element of learning. This type of feedback is focused on individual pupils, and requires the teacher to spend time with each pupil. Whether this is practical in a large class of over 30 must be ascertained. It certainly needs to be located within a carefully planned programme which allows for individual pupil/ teacher interaction regularly. In extending Black and Wiliam's (1998) and Kluger and DeNisis' (1996) recognition that students are likely to use feedback in different ways, Hattie and Jaeger (1998: 117) emphasise that students will often bias feedback in order to support their own beliefs. But more importantly they highlight the importance of teachers trying to establish how individuals have interpreted feedback. They state 'excellent teaching involves being aware of individual students' dispositions to receiving feedback information'.

Perrenoud (1998: 87) also contends that the effectiveness of feedback lies ultimately with the pupil.

> Thus we must concede that some of the messages which the teacher conceives as feedback do not in fact play this role for the pupil, because their form, their tone, their content (verbal or non-verbal), the moment chosen, the point reached in the work and the interactive situation in which they occur do not allow the pupils to understand them or 'do something with them'.

Perrenoud draws together the notion that feedback is part of self-regulation with its role in advancing learning. He considers the relationship between self-regulation (specifically feedback) and learning and suggests that processes of self-regulation do not necessarily have learning process as their objective. However, regulation can affect learning. The way in which this may occur is not easy to ascertain.

It is difficult to ascertain at which point in time and under what conditions the regulation of the activity induces effects in the learning process. In between what the pupil does and what passes through his or her mind, the mediations are complex. And what happens in the mind does not necessarily affect learning.

(Perrenoud 1998: 88–9)

Seeking to establish a connection between self-regulation and learning development is part of the argument so far developed in this chapter. However, beyond this is the view that understanding learning, through processes which can form part of assessment, can have an impact on learning.

The elements of self-regulation which have been discussed – self-efficacy, motivation, metacognition and feedback – can all be aspects of learning, whether for self-regulation or not. They can form part of the ways in which pupils influence and exercise control of their learning, and how they make sense of their experiences and build upon them. Furthermore, they can be used in the way they understand their learning, make judgements about it and decide the way forward. At this level, assessment and learning become part of the same process. They are interlocked in the development process. If this is the case, the notion that assessment should be a component of learning rather than merely a measure of it, needs to be further developed. Processes which may influence teaching are therefore likely to influence assessment and vice versa. Strategies which may encourage children to consider their learning more carefully and help them close the gap in their learning or to bridge the gap (Vygotsky) need to be considered from the perspectives of both teaching and learning. Constructivist theory highlights the importance of the pupils' role in making sense of learning. Implicitly from this perspective is the view that pupils must also be able to make judgements about their learning through assessment – self-assessment. The processes which would be necessary for this to occur are also important for the development of learning. Pupils' role in self-assessment can thus be seen as a form of learning. This readily permits the view that assessment can be regarded *as* learning. This is a particular form of assessment, located in a formative framework and not necessarily related to agreed standards.

The remainder of this chapter will try to set out key aspects for consideration when developing self-assessment. It draws from the case study in the previous chapter and from the aspects of self-regulation already outlined in this chapter.

Developing self-assessment

Assumptions

For pupils to be encouraged to engage in the process of self-assessment within the primary classroom there are a number of assumptions which need to be made explicit before more practical ideas and possible principles for development are outlined. They are drawn from the case study analysis and theoretical considerations presented so far.

1   Pupils must be seen as active learners who are active in the process of interpreting and constructing their learning.
2   Pupils know that their views of their own work as well as their judgements and comments are welcomed by the teacher.
3   Pupils must have some developing awareness that they have a role in shaping and changing their own learning.
4   Pupils must have some notion that their learning is part of a process of development which has defined steps which the teacher will outline.
5   Pupils' learning is situated within a particular context which must be accounted for in the self-assessment process.
6   Factors related to pupil self-efficacy and motivation will impact on the way a pupil engages with the self-assessment process.
7   Self-assessment involves the use of skills which pupils at the primary school age are still developing, such as metacognition.
8   Pupil involvement in self-assessment in the primary age phase is part of the process of developing skills not just a limited application of already learnt skills.
9   The outcomes of self-assessment of pupils at the primary age phases will have limited relevance or validity in contexts beyond the classroom.
10 The process of self-assessment may have benefits to pupils beyond the assessment process, if regarded as a form of learning as well as a form of assessment.

The purpose(s) of self-assessment

The possible purposes outlined here which may propel the use of self-assessment are not given with any indication of priority. Indeed the purposes cited for developing and using self-assessment are likely to combine a number of issues. Their emphases are likely to relate to whether reference is being made to a specific self-assessment occasion or to the principal of self-assessment as part of general priority and policy. Purposes of self-assessment, within the constructions which are being developed here, include the following:

1   As a tool for formative assessment.
2   As a tool for summative assessment (the focus of self-assessment for summative purposes in the primary age phase is likely to be mainly within a defined context (the classroom) rather than for more general accountability purposes and put alongside other forms of evidence which it may help to qualify).
3   As an aspect of learning development providing information about the gap between what has been learnt and what needs to be learnt.
4   To enable targets to be set, linked to current achievements.
5   To enable pupils to think about their own learning, thus encouraging the development of metacognition.
6   To provide a forum for pupils and teachers to talk about their work.
7   For pupils to be able to be actively involved in curriculum and assessment practices (i.e. their learning).
8   To form part of the developing process of self-regulation which continues throughout lifelong learning.

From these purposes it is clear that the relationships between learning and assessment are tightly interconnected.

The practices of pupil self-assessment

Having clarified assumptions and purposes for pupil self-assessment some strategies for implementation are offered. The suggestions made are offered in general terms so that they can be applied to a variety of contexts. Elements for consideration are drawn from the experiences outlined in the previous chapter. These looked at a case study in which self-assessment was developed, as well as from the theoretical considerations already outlined in terms of learning theories. Points for consideration in the practice of self-assessment in the primary classroom are offered under the following six themes:

1   creating the classroom context;
2   understanding learning;
3   making judgements;
4   recognising differences;
5   closing the gap;
6   moving on.

Creating the classroom context

Developing self-assessment strategies in the classroom cannot be seen in isolation from other classroom activities and practices. The active role which pupils need to assume during self-assessment should also be evident in other aspects of classroom experience. The skills required to be effective in self-assessment need to be supported and developed throughout the curriculum. Vygotsky claims that the basis of language and thought starts with the social.

> Every function in the child's cultural development appears twice: first on the social level, and later, on the individual level; first between people (interpsychological), and then inside the child (intrapsychological). This applies equally to voluntary attention, to logical memory, and to the formation of concepts. All the higher psychological functions originate as actual relations between human individuals.
>
> (Vygotsky 1978: 57)

Following Vygotsky's contention, the levels of higher order thinking required in self-assessment need to be developed as social practices before they can be internalised by a pupil. Thus, there seems to be a strong case for trying to ensure that higher order thinking skills feature as part of classroom interactions. Lipman (1991) advocates that the classroom should be a community of inquiry. In such an environment classroom discussion in which pupils ask each other questions, offer reasons, listen and respond to each other's points of view and seek to identify each other's assumptions, are all important aspects of cooperative activity. The teacher's role in facilitating and guiding such inquiry is not one of dominance but of discerned nurturing, encouraging pupils to interact and engage with ideas and concepts in ways which will foster thought and reflection. If pupils are not encouraged to participate within their learning environment, in interactions with one another and with the teacher, in ways which promote higher order thinking skills, then their involvement in self-assessment is unlikely to be of value. Features which might characterise a community of inquiry, whether as part of specific curriculum subjects or as discrete learning opportunities, include:

- seeking and explaining logical relationships between items of knowledge;
- asking appropriate questions;
- highlighting possible assumptions for different perspectives;
- exploring a variety of possibilities;
- explaining the limits of a concept or idea;
- identifying or discovering criteria;
- seeking alternative views and solutions;
- asking for and developing reasons;
- making considered judgements;
- drawing relevant distinctions and inferences from information;
- trying to anticipate possible consequences of particular scenarios.

All the skills here are ones which can be developed throughout schooling. Within the primary classroom, encouragement of their development will be only the start of the process. More consolidated and extended development can be enhanced as pupils' cognitive competencies increase.

The process of involving pupils actively in thinking about their learning and discussing concepts should also foster a sense of valuing pupils' ideas. This is a fundamental requirement within pupil self-assessment. The whole process of self-assessment needs to be founded upon a sense of trust. Pupils must feel that the judgements they make and ideas that they share will be used positively by teachers. The consequences of their being honest and open about the way they have worked, as well as the product of their efforts, must be seen to be fair. If pupils perceive that any comments they make about their work relating to weaknesses or aspects for improvement have negative consequences (such as redoing work, extending the work, completing as homework) they are unlikely to be forthcoming with such comments. It is therefore important for pupils to

understand the possible impact and status of what they are invited
to engage. Furthermore, if the judgements which pupils make are
merely overruled by a teacher's judgements then they will consider
little point in offering their opinion. Trying to balance pupils'
views of their learning with the teacher's more directive agenda
and informed perspective requires careful consideration. (This is
developed more specifically in pp. 135–8, in the section headed
'Recognising and acknowledging differences'.)

Understanding learning

The case study outlined in the previous chapter illustrated the use of
self-assessment initiatives with Years 5 and 6 pupils. Both formative
and summative approaches were used. The attempt to involve pupils
in summative self-assessment of research skills and attitudes at the
end of a topic was highlighted as being rather a bolt-on process.
What was not clear from the pupils' responses was the extent to
which they had drawn on the full range of experiences or whether
their results were based on a memorable selection of their work
which may or may not represent what had been undertaken. The
pupils' judgements do, however, reflect their overall judgement of
their skills and attitudes which extracts what is salient for them. In
order to help pupils consider the breadth of their learning experiences throughout a topic, more regular opportunities to consider
their work and involvement may assist in offering further steps which
can be built up and synthesised for a final summative self-assessment.

The main focus of the pupil self-assessment in the case study cited
was on formative assessment which was linked to individual lessons.
Part of the rationale for the practices developed was built on the basis
that the learning criteria for each lesson should be made clear to
the pupils as part of the teaching element of the lesson. Criteria for
each lesson were made explicit and attempts made to illustrate how
such criteria could be translated into the work requested for the
lesson. The lessons, thus, had clearly defined objectives which were
translated into criteria that were the subject of discussion and
understanding in the early part of each lesson. The intention was to
develop a shared understanding of learning aims between the pupil
and the teacher. Furthermore, the criteria were designed to form
the focus for the self-assessment so that judgements and comparisons could be made between teacher and pupil. As indicated in
the previous chapter, there were limitations with this aspect of the

development of the initiative. It was clear that the criteria were not always fully considered by the pupils when undertaking or assessing their work. Furthermore, pupils also included personal factors which were not related to the criteria such as effort, the standard of their previous work as well as how they compared their work with that of other pupils in their self-assessments.

The case study showed that the use of criteria had been of importance to some of the children. The example of Jason showed that the focus on specific criteria in each lesson had enabled him to recognise his developing skills which had previously been overshadowed by specific language difficulties. Having specific criteria permitted him to push his other difficulties to one side and to see beyond them. Other children in the case study had indicated in the pupil interviews that the criteria had helped them to understand what was important in a task. This had been identified as helpful by the pupils. It seems to support the view already expressed in the research (e.g. Black and Wiliam op. cit.) that supporting pupils through task-related issues is more effective than supporting them in more general positive ways.

In recognising this point, it was also clear from the case study data that many of the children had attempted to use the criteria alongside their own agendas for work and success. They were trying to make sense of their new learning in their own way. From the learning theories already outlined throughout this book, the importance of recognising that pupils' learning is embedded in a context which includes the social, and is related to previous learning, should not be overlooked. If pupils are to be encouraged to articulate something of their learning through self-assessment, trying to force sole reference to objective criteria may not be desirable or helpful.

The use of criteria in the process of self-assessment is none the less considered to be of value. They will certainly need to feature in the teacher's agenda for teaching and learning. In order to satisfy both school-based and national accountability demands clear criteria must be articulated as part of the comprehensive plan of curriculum coverage. The assumption that a particular form of effective teaching will result in pupils fulfilling these criteria, which can then be easily assessed, promotes a distorted and grossly naive picture of the complexities of the teaching and learning process. It is within such a framework that any developments in self-assessment are located and developed. However, any intention that self-assessment should contribute to a similar purpose of accountability will falsely reduce its practice to a level of objectivity which is neither feasible nor desirable and which fails to account for both the ways in which pupils learn and how they understand their learning.

The extent to which pupils can make sense of criteria which form the basis of teaching and the focus for learning will be partly related to the level of their cognitive development. The extent to which pupils in the primary age phase can use criteria objectively increases in the junior phases of schooling (over 7 years old, according to Piaget's model). The complexity of the criteria as well as the way in which they relate to and build upon existing knowledge and experiences are also significant factors. Pupils' use of criteria within the curriculum may be varied. For example within maths or science their use may be related to classification and setting – to help children see relationships and recognise inclusiveness. This is likely to be related to known factors which have been part of knowledge development and require application, consolidation and manipulation. Pupils' use of criteria in terms of framing a task and assessing it requires similar skills but is likely to be related to knowledge, skills and understanding which is new and developing. The focus of the criteria, however, are likely to be in what Vygotsky terms the ZPD (see Chapter 2). Thus, the way that pupils may be able to consider them and relate them to their own thinking and performance is likely to be more problematic. As pupils continue through the primary years the challenge of using task criteria in the context of self-assessment seems to be as relevant to the substance of curriculum experience as it is to the understanding of their learning through assessment. Thus, the curriculum challenge which self-assessment may provide should not be overlooked. Appropriate teacher guidance and support, however, is crucial.

Recognising the role of task criteria as part of the basis for self-assessment involves acknowledging that any such criteria will be embedded in the context of learning and individual interpretations of that learning. The way that criteria are shared with pupils must try to encourage them to make connections between what pupils already know and what is being asked of them. The criteria must therefore be shared in a way which allows application and interpretation rather than in a closed form which assumes universal interpretation. Following this, teachers need to try to find out how pupils have understood what the task requires. Trying to establish this information is an important part of formative assessment for the teacher. Without an attempt to understand how pupils perceive the curriculum, and what sense they make of it, there will be little hope of gaining relevant insights into the process of learning or gaining any information which might contribute to its further enhancement. The process of pupil self-assessment should be an enabling process which supports pupils in articulating their priorities and their views of the tasks that they have undertaken. From this basis pupils can consider the work they have done and try to formulate a judgement about what has been achieved.

Making judgements

The case study cited in the previous chapter illustrated how pupils were required to use an A to E grading system as part of their self-assessment. This was popular with the pupils since they seemed to think that grades offered status. The pupils' perceptions here are obviously linked to the way in which they have understood other assessment systems, and the status which they appear to have been given. In the case study school illustrated, grades were frequently used by the teachers which may have promoted the eagerness of pupils to use them. Their currency was evidently high. Within the national educational arena the use of levels for the attainment targets offers a similar type of assessment score output. Although the levels are based on criteria which are consolidated in level descriptions, the overall assessment result is simply conveyed in a single number. Critical for consideration in deciding how best to summarise and communicate assessments are the purposes to which they are to be used. In the national assessment system, since its development, the emphasis has been increasingly on providing summative assessment information for national accountability. Having assessment results which are simple is important if large amounts of data are to be collated and compared. In the case study, there was a clear dilemma about the purposes of the self-assessment. There was a sense in which national trends in assessment should be followed, but with an added voice – that of the pupil. Thus, the decision to use grades in the self-assessment process was designed to make the self-assessment results suitable for inclusion as part of school accountability as well as for formative class-based assessments. It seems (as with national assessment developments which sought to serve both formative and summative assessments) that the irreconcilable cannot be reconciled (drawing on Nutall's statement that the National Curriculum claimed to reconcile the irreconcilable). It was clear that the pupils were drawing on a variety of sources of evidence and interpreting the grades in their own ways. Trying to claim that the self-assessment grades offered reliable evidence for summative assessment would have little foundation. Pupils admitted in their interviews that the basis for their grades was not always related to the criteria. Furthermore, for pupils who did indicate that they tried to use the criteria, the use of the grades tended to focus on selected criteria and not represent the full picture. It seemed that the use of grades offered little to the self-assessment system, except for the status which pupils associated with them.

Pupils were encouraged to consider the criteria which had been outlined for the task and then to link these criteria with the grade range given to them. This structure offered pupils an additional level of abstraction in dealing with the assessment. It seemed to further remove the pupils from the heart of what they were assessing. The grades, which were recorded, were thus supposed to represent the judgement made of the criteria. However, the grades gave no information about the specific criteria for the task. Thus, in terms of providing information for further improvements and development, there was very little useful information recorded. This does not mean, however, that the pupils and the teacher did not benefit from the process of discussing and considering the work assessed: the process carried out during the process of self-assessment provides more meaningful information which can be sustained and utilised despite the more limited records.

The process of self-assessment is based on pupils making at least one judgement on their work. The capacity which pupils have to control the factors that influence their judgements will vary according to their age and experience. As pupils move through the primary age phase their ability to deal with more complex issues as well as more abstract ones increases (e.g. Hacker 1998 op. cit.). Pupils' skills in self-assessment during the primary phase must, therefore, be seen as developmental. In seeking to involve pupils in the process of making judgements about their work some consideration must be given to ways of guiding them in this process so that their skills can be extended and enhanced. The potential for self-assessment to contribute to the curriculum rather than just respond to it should not be overlooked.

Looking more closely on the possible pathway of skills which pupils may use for self-assessment offers some insight into the level in which self-assessment may both draw upon and develop pupils' thinking and reasoning skills. Figure 6.1 offers some possible

A

What are the relevant factors?
(e.g. Task criteria, comparison to previous and other pupils' work, effort, interest, motivation self-efficacy.)

Remembering
Recalling
Comparing
Prioritising
Synthesising
Distinguishing
Associating
Applying

B

What judgements could I make?

Hypothesising
Choosing
Defining
Comparing
Contrasting
Deducing

C

What are the consequences of each?

Inferring
Predicting
Surmising

D

What judgements will my peers have? What judgements might my teacher have? What judgement do I want? What is fair?

Classifying
Generalising
Prioritising

E

Judgement (best possible option)

Deducting
Comparing
Contrasting
Using evidence
Deciding
Prioritising
Choosing
Ranking

Figure 6.1 Judgement and skill in pupil self-assessment.

components of the process of making an assessment judgement as part of pupil self-assessment and suggests possible skills (given in italics) which may be used at each stage.

The stages A to E identified in this module are not intended to promote a neat sequential and linear process for self-assessment. Consideration of the five stages included may partly be simultaneous; their combination and priority may differ for different pupils on different assessment occasions. Furthermore, the skills used at each stage will differ. The reasons for the difference in the use of skills will vary and might include the following:

- Cognitive ability of the pupil limits the extent to which cognitive and metacognitive skills can be utilised.
- Cognitive ability may influence the extent to which pupils can consider and work with multiple variants at any one time, thus affecting the range of skills which might be utilised in the self-assessment processes.
- Issues related to motivation and/or self-efficacy may influence the way in which skills are used.
- Favoured priorities, personal preferences and the values and assumptions held are all likely to influence the way in which a pupil interprets each stage.

Thus the pathway a pupil may take in the process of making self-assessment judgements may be extremely simple (conceptually), based on loosely substantiated choices informed mainly by personal preferences. On the other hand, the process may use a range of metacognitive processes which are clearly defined and rationally utilised. These two scenarios are not offered as a continuum, even though the pupils are likely to function in the process of self-assessment somewhere between them. Although the emphasis which is developed in this chapter stresses the need for participation in self-assessment to be developmental, as cognitive skills are enhanced through a range of learning activities, there is also recognition that sharpened cognitive skills will not result in a uniform process of self-assessment. Any self-assessment initiative which assumes uniformity of practice may mislead, particularly if there is an assumption that pupils can be steered to think in particular ways about their work.

If we are to accept that pupils will draw on a variety of sources of evidence and make decisions which are informed from several perspectives, then a key part of self-assessment must be in examining the processes used as well as the outcomes presented. In terms of gaining and making sense of a self-assessment judgement, it must be acknowledged that this judgement will be based on a number of decisions, each of which may have drawn on different evidence and involved different skills. Trying to ensure that pupils are encouraged to articulate the basis for their judgements should feature as part of the self-assessment processes. Thus, in addition to the ever increasing number of self-assessment sheets which encourage pupils to offer their judgements on aspects of their work, some consideration of how these judgements have been made will be of use. Such encouragement would enhance the way in which the self-assessments information could be understood and subsequently used. Figure 6.2 is offered as an example. It is presented in a way which illustrates principles for development rather than a sheet which will serve any particular pupil group.

For pupils to work with such questions assumes that they are already familiar with being engaged in tasks which require them to think and to reflect. The questions posed in this example may be the focus of a discussion session rather than presented in written form. The aim is to try to elicit the reasons behind the judgements pupils make so that perceptions and thinking about learning are understood alongside the pupils' work. This should enhance the ways in which both pupil and teacher make sense of and subsequently build upon existing learning.

Recognising and acknowledging differences

The self-assessment process outlined here seeks to stimulate thinking about learning which is not designed to reduce assessment to simple objective measures. In seeking to enable pupils to present a range of factors which they consider have influenced their work, teachers, potentially, may have a complex task of helping pupils and themselves to meaningfully combine and interpret the information. There is no assumption that assessment information will be transparent and easy to produce or to use by either pupil or teacher. It may well be that the judgements which teachers make about a pupil's achievements during a lesson may not fully concur with those made by the pupil. If teaching and learning are to successfully interrelate there must be some attempt to recognise, understand and work with differences. The following headings (after Figure 6.2) offer a framework, which may help in this task.

Thinking about my work?

What is important to me in this activity?

	Very important	Important	Slightly important	Not important
The criteria for the lesson				
Whether I have finished the task				
How much effort I put into it				
How my work looks compared to somebody else's				
Whether I enjoyed doing it				
Whether it is a good piece of work for me				
Whether it is not a good piece of work for me.				

What two judgements could you make about your work in this lesson? What do you think the consequences will be of making either?

My judgement about my work today	Consequences of making this judgement
1	
2	

What are the reasons for each of these judgements? Try to think of two reasons for each judgement

	Reason 1	Reason 2
Judgement 1		
Judgement 2		

What are the pros and cons of making each judgement?

	Pros	Cons
1st possible judgement		
2nd possible judgement		

How fair are your judgements?

1

2

What judgements do you think your teacher will make of this activity?

Your decision

Weigh up all the factors

What did you do best in this activity?

What things are you not so happy with?

Have you any ideas of what you need to do next to improve?

Figure 6.2 Promoting pupil thinking in assessment and learning.

- **Articulating** – A conscious effort needs to be paid to ensuring that pupils have appropriate opportunities to express the factors which have influenced their work. A pupil's self-assessment may be in written or spoken form, working individually, with a partner or in a group. Consideration should be given to the skills and abilities a pupil has to express his/her thinking. Thus, as with most aspects of the curriculum, facilitating pupils to participate in self-assessment will require differentiated tasks based on teacher knowledge of pupils' developing skills, capacities and attitudes.
- **Acknowledging** – Even if a pupil's view of his/her work is at odds with the teacher's impression it is important that the pupil's assessment is valued. The pupil's own view of progress and achievement will be the starting point for his or her future learning. Seeking to overrule or dismiss this view is unlikely to be conducive to future learning.
- **Agreeing** – In the case study presented in the previous chapter there was an attempt to formulate an agreed grade, supposedly drawing from both the teacher's and pupil's initial judgements. In reality, it tended to be the teacher offering a decisive judgement without an exchange of reasons or clear deliberation. The value of such an 'agreed grade' was thus in question. Furthermore, the focus on a grade as the focal point of the agreement seemed unhelpful. An essential part of 'agreeing' is accepting each other's viewpoint as potentially useful for moving on.

Closing the gap

If pupils have offered judgements about their work, these provide a useful starting point for discussion and for helping the child to begin to progress. If the process of self-assessment deliberately seeks to ensure that different perspectives of achievement are sought, it potentially, on the surface, makes the task of synthesising information, so that future steps can be taken, seem more difficult. Such difficulty is identified only in comparison to systems which seek to oversimplify assessment and learning processes.

Pupil learning, ultimately, falls with the child. If a child is unwilling, or is not able to connect with the ideas and tasks presented then little or no learning will take place. The judgements which may be made within a self-assessment experience may or may not (in the teacher's eyes) be the most appropriate to serve the further development of learning considered appropriate. The teacher's power and responsibility for controlling, and being accountable for, the curriculum and the quality of teaching (measured in our current system by pupil achievement) may not always sit easily alongside pupils' priorities and perceptions. By giving pupils a voice through pupil self-assessment there needs to be a carefully considered approach to trying to integrate perspectives. Even though curriculum criteria may well have been identified during both teaching and assessment processes, as already indicated, many primary pupils are highly likely to have prioritised additional considerations. A strategy for trying to combine these views may be to ensure that the final agreement covers both curriculum achievements in their broadest sense (i.e. including personal and social factors)

It will be desirable for teachers to use pupil's judgements as a starting point and to incorporate other judgements as appropriate. Thus, part of the teacher's role should be to affirm some/all of the judgements already made as well as to augment or add to them. This will help the pupils to reconsider and expand their reflections about their learning. With the help of discussion with the teacher, pupils may be able to gain new insights into the ways that they have carried out their work and how they need to further develop it. Drawing once again from Vygotsky's work, the role of another who is more knowledgeable seems just as appropriate in the assessment process as in the process of learning. Thus, to leave self-assessment as a confined activity for each individual is limiting. Its potential lies as part of the wider processes of assessment which attempts to connect teaching and learning for both the teacher and the pupil.

The discussion which follows self-assessment has the scope to value pupil perspectives, to augment them, and to offer feedback which has a known starting point. From such discussions the pupil can try to discern whether there are some points which can be highlighted as targets for the future.

Moving on

Moving on from one assessment experience to another should not be a large leap but part of a continuum. Although the nature of the curriculum content may sometimes appear to have few connections, as topics change and new themes are pursued, the way in which pupils make sense of their progress will impact on subsequent learning experiences. In the case study offered in the previous chapter, pupils were asked, in negotiation with the teacher, to construct mini-targets. The intention here was to highlight specific targets, which the children could understand and act upon in their subsequent learning. Part of the problem identified with this aspect of the case study was the way in which the mini-targets tended to be identified by the teacher. Some of the children had found it difficult to recall their targets and had evidently prioritised their own issues for development. A further consideration related to the focus of the targets. If they are specifically linked to tasks then their relevance to subsequent learning may be marginal. Trying to make targets more general so that they can form the focus for the future is more difficult – particularly if the pupils are to help formulate them. Nevertheless, if self-assessment is to contribute to formative assessment both pupils and teachers need to be able to link the assessments to future learning. For children to be able to move on in their areas of weakness or to consolidate aspects of uncertainty they must be able to begin to make connections between where they are and where they intend to be. Trying to crystallise this step is as important for the pupils in making the step of learning as it is for the teacher who seeks to plan the curriculum appropriately. From Kluger and DeNisi's (1996) research, mentioned earlier, pupils will decide the extent to which they respond to feedback and the targets related to them. Additionally, as Hattie and Jaeger (1998) emphasise, they will bias the feedback to support their own beliefs. Thus, the understanding which pupils have of what they should aim for next is likely to be the key factor in the way in which they learn. Pupils' willingness to seek out new directions in their learning, to be motivated to achieve new things and to work at skills which are hitherto not fully understood, will depend on the way in which they perceive their capacity to succeed. As previously mentioned, motivation and self-efficacy are important aspects of self-regulated processes of which learning is a part. Targets, constructed in a supportive context stressing pupil approval, participation and understanding, may well be instrumental – even pivotal – in facilitating the learning process.

Conclusion

This chapter has argued for greater involvement of pupils in the assessment processes which should be seen as an integral part of their learning. The involvement of primary pupils in the self-assessment process is highlighted as complex, involving a variety of skills, which are both developed and utilised in the processes. Rationalised from a theoretical position and supported from insights gleaned from school-based initiatives this chapter has presented a case for the further development of pupil assessment in a way which reinterprets assessment – as learning.

Chapter 7

Assessment *as* learning

A number of principles and concepts have been suggested as a basis for promoting assessment *as* learning. Specifically, emphasis has been placed on exploring the process of pupil learning. Pupil participation has been recognised as central to learning, with the processes of self-regulation and understanding being equally fundamental. Whereas much research and discussion have linked formative assessment to ways in which teachers have tried to inform their own practice so that pupils' needs are more specifically met, there has been little sustained analysis of the ways in which pupils participate in this process. Without their goodwill and their continued commitment to learning, there will be little chance of learning progressing. Pupils are often incorporated into the discussion on assessment as users of assessment information – through processes such as feedback. There is little account taken of the ways in which assessment processes (rather than outcomes) influence learning processes. Those that do exist tend to highlight adverse stress-related pressures linked to summative tests – usually through the popular press. Although the concerns raised should have an important place in our research and thinking they should not be at the expense of other strands of inquiry which endeavour to look beneath the surface of experiences dominated by national summative assessment systems.

Preparing for tests

Part of the argument offered in this book (Chapters 2 and 3) highlights the way in which both the National Curriculum and its accompanying assessments are grounded in assumptions about teaching and learning, stemming from models of behaviourism and technical rationality. The tendency is to prioritise outcomes rather than processes; focusing debate on effective teaching rather than effective learning. Chapter 4 highlights the case of Year 6 – which by many teachers' accounts is hijacked by the demands of national tests. On the surface, it offers an example of the impact of high stakes testing on classroom practice. Madaus' (1988) seven principles (Chapter 4), characterising measurement driven instruction (MDI), feature significantly in the way that Year 6 is often perceived. Teachers expressed their concern that the normal curriculum was suspended so that test revision could be undertaken for most of the year. In endeavouring to make sense of what characterised revision it was clear that although new curriculum input considerably diminished, aspects of test preparation in no way reflected a curriculum which was not promoting learning. The 'hurry along curriculum' (Dadds 1999) which seemed to characterise curriculum planning and delivery within the framework of the National Curriculum slowed down. In its place came a number of opportunities: to revisit concepts, skills and ideas in order to check for understanding; to encourage repetition so as to aid consolidation; to offer new contexts in which ideas can be considered and further developed; to encourage different and new connections to be made between aspects of learning; and to reflect on the ways in which learning has progressed. Rather than seeing this as suspending the curriculum it should be regarded as an important curriculum focus which facilitates learning in ways that are often overlooked when the rapid pace and progression of the curriculum emphasises content.

In the context of Year 6 teaching and learning, which seems driven by the demands of the end of Key Stage 2 tests, to advocate that test preparation practices may well exemplify good practice in teaching and learning may seem perverse. Indeed the examples given in Chapter 4 are intended to highlight possible insights rather than in any way seeking to present a *fait accompli*. The illustrations given from the focus group of teachers help to give some interpretation of the context of Year 6. They offer possible strategies for making what teachers feel to be the essential aspects of preparation in Year 6 more meaningful. Beyond this, strategies are offered which try to locate the demands of test preparation within a particular framework of pupil learning. The attempt to link practices (KS 2 testing and test preparation) that are grounded in one set of principles and ideologies (objectives model, accountability, standards, marketisation, behaviourism), with a framework which draws on very different principles (constructivism, metacognition, self-regulation), rests on a particular assumption. That is, that teachers are able to mediate the influences around them with their own practice. This is further developed later in this concluding chapter within the context of professionalism. Furthermore, it is suggested that an understanding of pupil learning should be the primary influence in considerations of teaching and assessment. Of course, what is promoted throughout this book is a particular view of learning which is developed and related to assessment. There are no claims made as to 'truth'; only to examining what seems to make sense from the realities of classroom life, from pupils' responses and from engagement with the growing body of research which exists in the field. Within the context of Year 6 teaching and learning the appeal is to recognise revision as providing valuable opportunities for deep learning, which seem seldom possible within the hurried pace of the National Curriculum in other years.

There are of course limitations, in that the focus of revision will be limited to the curriculum which is expected to form the content of the national tests. Whether similar periods, when the teaching of new information is suspended in other subject areas, would offer valuable learning opportunities needs to be considered – perhaps not in Year 6. Pupils' responses to lessons which focus on ideas previously known to them can be very varied. Many will often comment – 'we've done this before' whereas others will not be confident that they remember. However, when revision is presented in the context of test preparation it seems to be accepted. Pupils seem to grasp something of its importance because of the emphasis placed on the need for test success. However, outside the test context the need for revisiting ideas and concepts may not be seen. Issues of motivation and interest seem to be of significance. These are certainly issues which need to be examined further. The pace at which the curriculum is delivered is for most pupils likely to create certain expectations and give them particular messages about learning, its content, and delivery. Trying to understand more about these assumptions in order to consider how pupils might interpret changes and repetitions requires some sustained exploration.

What is argued is that the process of revision is an important aspect of learning – quite apart from the test performance which it is intended to serve. Chapter 4 contains no details of the test results of the pupils which teachers have prepared and considered in the study carried out. Their results, as measured in terms of National Curriculum tests are not considered relevant to the argument here since the processes of learning developed may not be indicated through the level of achievement in national tests. There is no attempt here to measure children's learning as a result of the revision processes undertaken and pupils' responses to them. There is a need for in-depth research, which probes pupils' learning in more in-depth ways over a more sustained period of time. The extent to which the national tests themselves might promote learning is of additional interest. The anecdotal account of Daniel's response to the Key Stage 1 reading test given in Chapter 1 does indicate a level of learning – both for him and his family. It serves only as an illustration, yet it raises the question of the extent to which the national tests directly influence rather than just measure learning. This is an area which is considerably under-researched in the context of National Curriculum tests.

Self-assessment

The notion of assessment as learning is most notably promoted through the process of self-assessment. First, the principles for self-assessment are grounded in principles of constructive learning; second, the ways in which pupils try to make sense of their experiences are examined so that suggestions about developing processes for pupil participation can be further promoted. In the light of the analysis and discussion, it is argued that children's personal and cognitive development may be enhanced through their engagement with aspects of self-assessment. Thus, self-assessment forms part of the process of learning rather than merely a way of providing formative assessment evidence. Conceptually, the principles and practices are related to the pupil's self-regulative role in learning. Without acknowledgement of the many and complex ways in which pupils understand, interpret and make sense of the experiences around them, any notion of assessment will be impoverished. Although there are no guarantees that outcomes which embrace self-assessment will offer more than a glimpse of pupils' understanding and achievement, they can give opportunities for pupils to think, learn and judge in ways which can continually be developed throughout schooling – and beyond.

For teachers to take on board some of the ideas that have been presented requires more than an interest in practices for self-assessment. Trying to put into place procedures of self-assessment which pupils can respond to after lessons, whether regularly or sporadically, is not enough. The assumptions and purposes for self-assessment, which are crystallised in Chapter 6, need to form a foundation for developing effective self-assessment practices. The process of mediation, highlighted as necessary for interpreting the experience of Year 6 in a new way, is only part of what is needed if the ideas promoted in Chapters 5 and 6 are to be developed within the realities of the classroom. What is required from teachers is a particular view of professional identity and values which enables them to enter into reflective practice. These would need to be based on negotiated agreements and a recognition that the cultures with which they engage (school based, family based, local, national) are likely to be characterised more by difference than they are by accord. From this perspective, teachers need to construct priorities based on complex judgements, often affected by competing influences. Some further exploration of this professional stance is offered, since it is crucial if teachers are to consider innovations and practices in the current educational climate.

The 'modernised' teaching profession

Teaching has been high profile in recent years. Even when one escapes from the pressures of work to see the latest block-busting movies at the cinema, the government's recruitment drive for more teachers features in Dolby stereo – 'Those who can, teach'. The next step, one may suggest, is to have the application forms in the foyers, and interviews in the interval. But how will these bright dynamic prospective new teachers, who set out one evening to watch 'Titanic' and came home as aspiring teachers, be transformed? They may well be impressed with the promises and perspectives in the Green Paper. On the cover of the summary it states:

> We need good teachers, whose skills and dedication are recognised and respected. That means a first class profession, well led and well supported. It means backing high standards with high rewards, which recognise the talents of those who teach our children.
>
> (DfEE 1998b)

The promise of high status, good career structure, fast tracking, and pay rewards, may well seem appealing. However, when the reality of primary teacher training strikes with over 700 competencies to prove (DfEE, circular 4/98), the task may seem more daunting.

Such demands form the basis for the 'new' and 'modernised' teaching professional. How does assessment feature in the preparation of the new professional and the structure of the 'modernised' teaching profession? A whole section is devoted to monitoring, assessment, recording and accountability in circular 4/98. To complete their initial teacher training successfully teachers are required to demonstrate the following standards.

a. Assess how well learning objectives have been achieved and use this assessment to improve specific aspects of teaching.
b. Mark and monitor pupils' assigned classwork and home-work providing constructive oral and written feedback, and setting targets for pupils' progress.
c. Assess and record each pupil's progress systematically, including through focused observation, questioning, testing, marking and use of these records to:
    i. check that pupils have understood and completed the work set;
    ii. monitor strengths and weaknesses and use the infor-mation gained as a basis for purposeful intervention in pupils' learning;
    iii. inform planning;
    iv. check that pupils continue to make demonstrable progress in their acquisition of the knowledge, skills and understanding of the subject.
d. Be familiar with the statutory assessment and reporting requirements and know how to prepare and present informative reports to parents;
    [...]
g. Recognise the level at which a pupil is achieving and assess pupils consistently against attainment targets, where applicable, if necessary with guidance from an experienced teacher;
h. Understand and know how national, local comparative and school data, including National Curriculum test data, where applicable, can be used to set clear targets for pupils' achievement;
i. Use different kinds of assessment appropriately for different purposes, including National Curriculum and other stan-dardised tests, and baseline assessment where relevant.
                (DfEE circular 4/98 section C: 15)

There is a particular emphasis in parts d, g, h, i on ensuring that statutory assessments and other assessments linked to National Curriculum attainment targets are undertaken, understood and acted upon by those entering the profession. Additionally, parts a, b and c require those entering teaching to make judgements about pupils' achievements in relation to specific learning objectives and to use these to inform teaching and to feedback to pupils. These standards make it clear that judgements lie in the hands of the teachers and that aspects of the assessment process, such as feedback, are unproblematic. As with all the other standards identified there is no suggestion that appropriate theory about learning, teaching and assessment should be examined and understood and that practice might be related to it. How long these standards will remain is uncertain, since the Green Paper (1998) reduces most assessment practices to bureaucratic tedium which can easily be resolved through technology.

> Diagnosis of pupils' strengths and weaknesses can be improved by new computer software.
>
> (para 6: 13)

> Using specialist staff and new technology can help relieve teachers of the bureaucratic burden which, all too often, has distracted them from their core function of teaching children well. Electronic registers, assessment and recording systems . . . Have a part to play in freeing teachers to teach and improving the effectiveness of schools.
>
> (para 8: 13)

It thus seems that the task of assessment, as we move towards our 'modernised teaching profession', is considered mainly to be more of a technical problem which can now be more easily solved with improved computer software. However, there may be some promise in the tone of the 2001 Green Paper (Building on Success) since it states: 'We want teachers to be able to focus exclusively on their central professional tasks of teaching, preparation and assessing pupils' work and on their own professional development' (para 5.339: 73). Here there is a recognition that assessment is a central professional task. As part of the twenty-first century profession, which is outlined in the 2001 Green Paper, teachers need, on the one hand, to 'promote innovation and increasingly contribute, individually and collectively, to the progress of the service as a whole'. Additionally, they are required 'to exercise informed professional judgement, basing their decisions as far as possible on data and evidence and fully exploiting modern technology'. On the other hand, they should 'accept accountability, above all, for the results of their students' (para 5.5: 65). This last characteristic of the new teaching profession makes it very clear that teachers are responsible for the achievements of their pupils. There is no recognition of the many ways in which pupils may achieve, the different contexts and cultures which contribute to learning and the possibility that pupils can play a major part, with teacher aid, in regulating their learning.

The scope which is hinted at by the term 'innovation' seems to offer very little potential for teachers to develop their own practice, particularly in the context of assessment. Professional judgement is clearly related to data and evidence. There is an assumption here that information can clearly be linked to evidence and thus ideas of innovation or intuition are accorded little acknowledgement.

It is central to the argument in this book that teachers are competent, able and willing to transform assessment into a learning context as part of their own developing professionalism, both for themselves and for their pupils. However, in the context of so much educational change, much of which can be argued to have adversely affected teachers' professional status and control, the ways in which they are now able to engage with ideas involving innovation and change, need to be explored.

A professional context for innovation and intuition

Professional status, in its traditional sense, has tended to be linked to attempts to identify criteria for professionalism such as being self-governing, having its own code of ethics, having autonomy (e.g. Hoyle 1969; Hoyle and John 1995). Seeking to ascribe professional status to teachers under such models has always been problematic. There is an assumption that ideal professions exist from which such traits can be elicited (Johnson 1972). Furthermore, problems in contemporary society with which professions are expected to engage can be solved by the appropriate profession (Perucci 1976). Attempts to resolve the problem of definition and ascribe 'professional status' were broached with the introduction of the notion of the semi-profession (Etzioni 1969). This concept was considered to be particularly appropriate for teachers, nurses and social workers, who do not easily fit within the traditional criteria. But even this approach assumes that there are particular characterising features which must be fulfilled in order to gain professional status. In recent decades in which teachers' skills and competencies have more and more been centrally controlled, Ozga (1995: 22) contends:

> It is pointless . . . to try to establish whether or not teachers are professionals in some abstract, absolute sense. Professionalism is best understood in context. Critical analyses of professionalism do not stress the qualities inherent in an occupation but explore the value of the service offered by the members of that occupation to those in power.

In the 1970s and 1980s teachers' independence in the classroom was considered to be linked to concerns about educational standards. Changes in the way schools were funded and pupil places allocated gave rise to market principles which effectively set schools in competition with each other. This provided a platform from which central government could alter the way in which it sanctioned teachers and allowed them to form their own professional identity. This resulted in completely changing the power and authority relationships, through reforming principles, which began through marketisation and have now – under New Labour – been characterised by modernisation and transformation.

There is no longer a sense in which teachers can be seen as having authority over their occupational domains. Any appeal to teachers' independence and professionalism by the government, in Hargreave's (1994: 118) terms is merely 'a strategy for getting teachers to collaborate willingly in their own professional exploitation as more and more effort is extracted from them'. In a society in which teachers' knowledge is no longer seen as expert and their authority is now controlled through central government, the traditional notion of professionalism is no longer relevant. Yet it is clear from what happens in schools and classrooms that teachers are able to interpret and make sense of their practice in ways which are not necessarily controlled and restrained. Already it has been indicated that teachers are able to mediate in the classroom. They are able to consider that which is imposed on them and to consider the best ways to translate such requirements into their specific working contexts of teaching, learning and assessment. Such mediation is continual, requiring teachers to act upon new and developing agendas perpetually. This emphasises a process in which teachers must engage; one which demands constant consideration of their practice. It requires teachers to learn how best to transform classrooms in ways which will fulfil what is nationally required within their own individual constructions of teaching and learning. The teacher must operate within the school, recognising that it is his/her actions and practice that will create the contexts for learning. Their claims to professional practice seem to lie in the ways that this is fulfilled, so that the pressures of competitive and commercial interests, at an organisational level, do not adversely affect the processes of teaching and learning. The ways in which teachers operate must recognise diverse means of constructing practice. In recognising these differences and making judgements relating to what is considered the best decisions within the classroom, the teacher must continually be thinking and learning. In such a scenario, there will not be a static model of professional practice but one which reflects the teachers' continual efforts in learning and reflecting. Nixon *et al.* (1997: 17) characterises professionalism as 'emergent', emphasising teachers as learners.

> What we are trying to track is not a fully accomplished profes-
> sionalism, but a professionalism still in the making: an emergent
> professionalism that can only be inferred from disparate though
> highly significant sets of institutional practice and organisational
> structure.

From this perspective, the concept of mediation needs to go further. There must be an attempt to recognise the range of values evident in education (pluralism), which is in contrast to identifying specific 'professional values'. Central to the idea of the emergent profes-sional, therefore, is the practice of agreement-making. Agreements will be needed at different levels, among different participants. They will underlie any process of mediation. Central to this process, claim Nixon *et al.* (1997: 19) is the process of deliberation. Drawing from Dillon (1994) they contend that 'deliberation is the communicative process whereby "the question of right action in circumstance" is resolved'. Essential features of these deliberations, they claim, should include issues of purposefulness and inclusiveness. For teachers to grasp and develop a sense of professionalism in an educational context in which they are more fully controlled and deskilled, depends on a radical rethinking of the ways in which educational problems and contexts are defined and embraced by teachers. Forms of agreement seem to be more pivotal in the ways that diversity and difference are acknowledged. This holds true at all levels and with all those who participate in teaching and learning.

In the context of the arguments promoted in this book, the role which teachers take in considering the relationships which exist between teaching, learning and assessment is critical. Although the concepts and practical implications are very much related to class-room contexts, their foundations must also relate to professional practice. It is within the framework of the emergent professional, who seeks to recognise differences, to enter into dynamic engagement with learners based on processes of negotiation, agreement and collaborative learning ventures, that the developments should be seen. Nixon *et al.* (1997: 16) state that within the field of student learning the emergent professional should ideally be 'characterised by collaborative teaching and planning, negotiated learning and assessment (together with peer assessment and review and self assessment), co-ordinated, multi-agency curriculum development, and strong teacher-parent partnerships'. Dialogue with pupils and recognition that their stake in learning is dependent on their being encouraged to play an active and collaborative part in the learning process, is thus identified as a key component for the emergent professionalism. The principles, foundations and ideas promoted through the concept of assessment *as* learning not only relates comfortably to developing notions of teacher professionalism, but may help to enhance it. Underpinning both teacher development and pupil progress is the notion of learning. It is fundamental to the task of education. The notion of learning is central to the way in which assessment is constructed so that learning can be advanced. Further-more, it is central to the way in which teachers need to reflect and develop their own practice in the context of professional learning. Although government policy enforces the need for learning and makes claim to the intention to establish avenues for lifelong learning, principles for practice remain implicit and often obscure.

Conclusion

What this book has attempted is to tease out priorities upon which principles for learning should be grounded, and to relate these to forms and frameworks of assessment, both formative and summa-tive, in order to develop interconnections between teaching, learning and assessment. It seeks to try to transform practices in learning and assessment so that they are reconceptualised and seen as an integral part of one another. The message is not for teachers to find more time to develop yet another approach to assessment, but to reconceptualise their professional practice, based on the priority for developing both their own and pupil learning. In so doing, there is the potential to recognise the ways in which assessment is not merely an adjunct to teaching and learning but offers a process through which pupil involvement in assessment can feature as part of learning – that is, assessment *as* learning.

Bibliography

Alexander, R. (1992) *Policy and Practice in Primary Education*, London: Routledge.

Alexander, R., Rose, J. and Woodhead, C. (1992) *Curriculum Organisation and Classroom Practice in Primary Schools*, London: DES.

Arnold, M. (1910) *Reports on Elementary Schools 1852–1882*, London.

Atkinson, T. and Claxton, G. (eds) (2000) *The Intuitive Practitioner*, Buckingham: OUP.

Bandura, A. (1997) *Self-efficacy: The Exercise of Control*, New York: Freeman.

Barber, M. (1996) *The Learning Game*, London: Victor Gollancz.

Bash, C. and Coulby, D (1989) *The Education Reform Act*, London: Cassell.

Bastick, T. (1982) *Intuition: How We Think and Act*, John Wiley and Sons.

Bennett, N. (1976) *Teaching Styles and Pupil Progress*, London: Open Books.

Bennett, N., Desforges, C., Cockburn, A. and Wilkinson, B. (1984) *The Quality of Pupil Learning Experiences*, London: Lawrence Erlbaum Associates.

Benenson, J. and Dweck, J.P. (1986) 'The development of trait explanations and self-evaluations in the academic and social domains', *Child Development* 57: 1179–87.

Black, P. (1998) *Testing: Friend or Foe?*, London: Falmer.

Black, P. and Wiliam, D. (1998) 'Assessment and classroom learning', *Assessment in Education* 5(1): 7–74.

Bloom, B.S., Hastings, J.T. and Madaus, G.F. (eds) (1971) *Handbook on the Formative and Summative Evaluation of Student Learning*, New York: McGraw-Hill.

Boekaerts, M. and Niemivirta, M. (2000) 'Self-regulated learning: finding a balance between learning goals and ego protective goals', in M. Boekaerts, P.R. Pintrich and M. Zeidner (eds) *Handbook of Self-Regulation* (pp. 417–50), San Diego: Academic Press.

Broadfoot, P. (2000) 'Assessment and intuition', in T. Atkinson and G. Claxton (eds) *The Intuitive Practitioner* (pp. 199–219), Buckingham: OUP.

Broadfoot, P., and Pollard, A. (2000) 'The changing discourse of assessment policy', in A. Filer (ed.) *Assessment: Social Practice, Social Product*, London: RoutledgeFalmer.

Bruner, J.S. (1961) *The Process of Education*, Cambridge, MA: Harvard University Press.

Bruner, J.S. (1966) *Towards a Theory of Instruction*, Cambridge, MA: Harvard University Press.

Bruner, J. (1986) *Actual Minds, Possible Worlds*, Cambridge, MA: Harvard University Press.

Carver, C.S. and Scheier, M.F. (2000) 'On the structure of behavioural self-regulation', in M. Boekhaerts, P.R. Pintrich and M. Zeidner (eds) *Handbook of Self-Regulation* (pp. 41–84), San Deigo: Academic Press.

Cizek, G.I. (1997) 'Learning, achievement and assessment: constructs at a crossroads', in G.D. Phye (ed.) *Handbook of Classroom Assessment*, San Diego: Academic Press.

Clarke, S. (1996) 'The impact of national curriculum statutory testing at key stages 1 and 2 on teaching and learning and the curriculum', *British Journal of Curriculum and Assessment* 7(1): 12–18.

Claxton, G. (2000) 'The anatomy of intuition', in T. Atkinson and G. Claxton (eds) *The Intuitive Practitioner*, Buckingham: OUP.

Conner, C. (ed.) (1991) *Assessment and Testing in the Primary School*, London: Falmer.

Covington, M.V. (1998) *The Will to Learn*, Cambridge University Press.

Crahay, M. (1996) 'Learning to think or learning to memorize?' *Prospects* 26(1): 55–83.

Dadds, M. (1999) 'Some politics of pedagogy', paper presented at 'New Minds' Conference, St. Martin's College, Ambleside, March.

Dann, R. (1991) 'Pupil assessment in the primary school: with special reference to the assessment implications of the Education Reform Act 1988', unpublished PhD thesis, University of Southampton.

Dann, R. (1996a) 'Developing pupils' skills in self-assessment in the primary classroom', *Primary Practice 5* June: 4–13.

Dann, R. (1996b) 'Pupil self-assessment in the primary classroom: a case for action', *Education 3–13* 24(3): 55–60.

Dann, R. and Simco, N. (2000) 'Teachers in charge: a speculative vision for the future of primary education', *Education 3–13* 28(1): 36–40.

Daugherty, R. (1995) *National Curriculum Assessment: A Review of Policy 1987–1994*, London: Falmer.

Davis, A. (1998) *The Limits of Educational Assessment*, Oxford: Blackwell.

Dearing, R. (1993) *The National Curriculum and its Assessment: Final Report*, London: School Curriculum and Assessment Council.

Demetriou, A. (1989) 'Organisation and development of self-understanding and self-regulation: towards a general theory', in B.J. Zimmerman and D.H. Schunk (eds) *Self-Regulated Learning and Academic Achievement* (pp. 209–251), New York: Springer-Verlag.

Department of Education and Science (1985) *Better Schools*, London: HMSO.

Department of Education and Science (1987) *National Curriculum 5–16: A Consultation Document*, London: HMSO.

Department of Education and Science (1988a) *Task Group in Assessment and Testing: A Report*, London: HMSO.

Department of Education and Science (1988b) *Task Group on Assessment and Testing: 3 Supplementary Reports*, London: HMSO.

Department of Education and Science (1988c) *National Curriculum: English for Ages 5–11*, November, London: HMSO.

Department of Education and Science (1989) *Report on the Records of Achievement National Steering Committee*, January, London: HMSO.

Department for Education and Employment (1997) *Excellence in Schools*, London: HMSO.

Department for Education and Employment (1998a) Teaching: High Status, High Standards Circular 4/98. London: HMSO.

Department for Education and Employment (1998b) *Teachers: Meeting the Challenge of Change*, Green Paper, London: HMSO.

Department for Education and Employment (1999) *The National Curriculum for England*, London: HMSO.

Department for Education and Employment (2001) *Schools Building on Success*, Green Paper, London: HMSO.

Dewey, J. (1963) *Experience and Education*, London: Collier-Macmillan.

Dillon, J.T. (ed.) (1994) *Deliberation in Education and Society*, Norwood, NJ: Ablex.

Donaldson, M. (1978) *Children's Minds*, London: Fontana.

Edelman, G. (1987) *Neural Darwinisim – The Theory of Neuronal Group Selection*, New York: Basic Books.

Edwards, D. and Mercer, N. (1987) *Common Knowledge*, London: Methuen.

Eisner, E.W. (1969) In D. Lawton (1983) *Curriculum Studies and Educational Planning*, London: Hodder & Stoughton.

Elliott, J. (1988a) 'Education in the Shadow of G.E.R.B.I.L.', *Lawrence Stenhouse Memorial Lecture*, British Education Research Association Conference, University of East Anglia, September.

Elliott, J. (1988b) 'The State v Education: the challenge for teachers', paper presented to the *BERA National Curriculum Conference* 10 March, London: Institute of Education.

Elliott, J. (1989) 'Disconnecting knowledge and understanding from human values: a critique of National Curriculum Development', paper given at the *National Curriculum 'Moving into Focus' conference*, University of Liverpool Evaluation and Assessment Unit, April.

Elliott, J. (1998) *The Curriculum Experiment*, London: OUP.

Ericsson, K.A and Oliver, W.L. (1995) 'Cognitive skills', in N.J. Mackintosh and A.M. Coloman (eds) *Learning and Skills*, London: Longman.

Etzioni, A. (1969) *The Semi-Professions and their Organisations*, New York: Free Press.

Filer, A. (ed.) (2000) *Assessment: Social Practice, Social Product*, London: RoutledgeFalmer.

Fisher, R. (1990) *Teaching Children to Think*, London: Blackwell.

Forum (1988) 'The struggle continues' 3(3).

Galton, M. Simon, B. and Croll, P. (1980) *Inside the Primary Classroom*, London: Routledge & Kegan Paul.

Galton, M., Hargreaves, L., Cromber, C., Wall, D. with Pell, A. (1999) *Inside the Primary Classroom – 20 years on*, London: Routledge.

Gipps, C.V. (1994) *Beyond Testing*, London: Falmer.

Gipps, C.V., Brown, M., McCallum, B., McAlister, S. (1995) *Intuition or Evidence*, Buckingham: OUP.

Golby, M. (1989) 'Curriculum traditions', in B. Moon *et al.* (eds) *Policies for the Curriculum*, London: Hodder & Stoughton.

Gorman, R.A. (1977) *Dual Vision*, London: RKP.

Gould, F.G. (1880) *The Schoolmaster*, London.

Greeno, J., Moore, J., Smith, D. (1993) 'Transfer of situated learning', in D. Detterman and R. Sternberg (eds) *Transfer of Trial: Intelligence, Cognition and Instruction*, Norwood, NJ: Ablex.

Hacker, D.J. (1998) 'Definitions and empirical foundations', in D.J. Hacker, J. Dunlosky and A.C. Graesser (eds) *Metacognition in Educational Theory and Practice* (pp. 1–23), NJ: Lawrence Erlbaum Associates.

Hanson, F.A (2000) 'How tests create what they are intended to measure', in A. Filer (ed.) *Assessment: Social Practice, Social Product*, London: RoutledgeFalmer.

Hargreaves, A. (1994) *Changing Teachers, Changing Times: Teachers' Work and Culture in the Post Modern Age*, London: Cassell.

Harlen, W. and James, M. (1997) 'Assessment and learning: differences and relationships between formative and summative assessment', *Assessment in Education* 4(3): 365–79.

Hartley, D. (1997) *Re-schooling Society*, London: Falmer.

Hattie, J. and Jaeger, R. (1998) 'Assessment and classroom learning: a deductive approach', *Assessment in Education* 5(1): 111–22.

HMI (1991) *Assessment, Recording and Reporting*: A Report by HM Inspectorate on the first year, 1989–90, London: HMSO.

Hoyle, E. (1969) *The Role of the Teacher*, London: RKP.

Hoyle, E. and John, P.D. (1995) *Professional Knowledge and Professional Practice*, London: Cassell.

ILEA (1989) *Primary Language Record*, London.

Johnson, T.J. (1972) *Professions and Power*, London: Macmillan.

Kluger, A.N. and DeNisi, A. (1996) 'The effects of feedback interventions on performance: a historical review, a meta-analysis, and a preliminary feedback intervention theory', *Psychological Bulletin* 119: 254–84.

Lather, P. (1993) 'Fertile obsession: validity after poststructuralism', *Sociological Quarterly* 34(4): 673–93.

Lave, J. and Wenger, E. (1999) 'Legitimate peripheral participation', in P. Murphy (ed.) *Learners, Learning and Assessment*, London: PCP with OUP.

Lawton, D. (1983) *Curriculum Studies and Educational Planning*, London: Hodder & Stoughton.

Lipman, M. (1991) *Thinking in Education*, London: Falmer.

Lyotard, J.F. (1984) 'The postmodern condition' (trans. G. Bennington and B. Massumi), in D. Hartley (1997) *Re-Schooling Society* (pp. 26–7), London: Falmer.

Millerson, G. (1964) *The Qualifying Associations*, London: RKP.

Nelson, K., Plea, D. and Henseler, S. (1998) 'Children's theory of mind: an experiential interpretation', *Human Development* 41: 7–29.

Newman, D., Griffin, P. and Cole, M. (1989) *The Construction Zone: Working for Cognitive Change in School*, Cambridge University Press.

Nicholls, J.G. (1984) 'Achievement motivation: conceptions of ability, subjective experience, task choice and performance', *Psychological Review* 19: 308–46.

Nixon, J., Martin, J., McKeown, P. and Ranson, S. (1997) 'Towards a learning profession: changing codes of occupational practice within the new management of education', *British Journal of Sociology of Education* 18(1): 5–28.

Office for Standards in Education (OFSTED) (1993) *Well Managed Classes in Primary Schools*: Case studies of six teachers, London, HMSO.

Osborn, M., McNess, E. and Broadfoot, P. (2000) *Policy, Practice and Teacher Experience*, London: Continuum/Cassell.

Ozga, J. (1995) 'Deskilling a profession: professionalism, deprofessionalisation and the new managerialism', in H. Busher and R. Saran (eds) *Managing Teachers as Professionals* (pp. 21–37), London: Kogan Page.

Paris, S.G. and Byrnes, J.P. (1989) 'The constructivist approach to self-regulation and learning in the classroom', in B.J. Zimmerman and D.H. Schunk (eds) *Self-Regulated Learning and Academic Achievement* (pp. 169–200), New York: Springer-Verlag.

Pennycuick, D. (1988) 'The development, use and impact of graded tests', in R. Murphy and H. Torrance *The Changing Face of Educational Assessment*, Milton Keynes: OUP.

Perrenoud, P. (1998) 'From formative evaluation to a controlled regulation of learning processes. Towards a wider conceptual field', *Assessment in Education* 5(1): 85–102.

Perucci, R. (1976) 'In the service of Man', in J.E. Gerstl and G. Jacobs (eds) *Professions for the People*, New York: Schenkman.

Pintrich, P.R. (2000) 'The role of goal orientation in self-regulated learning', in M. Boekhaerts, P.R. Pintrich and M. Zeidner (eds) *Handbook of Self-Regulation* (pp. 451–502), San Diego: Academic Press.

Plowden Report (1967) *Children and Their Primary Schools*, Central Advisory Council for Education (England), London: HMSO.

Pollard, A. (1999) 'Towards a new perspective on children's learning?', *Education 3–13* 27(3): pp. 56–60.

Pollard, A. and Triggs, P. (2000) *Policy, Practice and Pupil Experience*, London: Continuum/Cassell.

Pollard, A., Broadfoot, P., Croll, P., Osborn, M. and Abbott, D. (1994) *Changing English Primary Schools?* London: Cassell.

Qualification and Curriculum Authority (1998a) *Standards at Key Stage 2 English, Mathematics and Science. Report of the 1997 National Curriculum Assessment of 11-year-olds*, January, London: HMSO.

Qualification and Curriculum Authority (1998b) *Maintaining Breadth and Balance at Key Stages 1 and 2*, London: HMSO.

Qualification and Curriculum Authority (2001) 'Key Stage 1, level three Reading Comprehension Test', *Diamonds*, London: HMSO.

Quicke, J. (1989) 'The "New Right" and education', in B. Moon *et al.* (eds) *Policies for the Curriculum*, London: Hodder & Stoughton.

Ray, R. (2001) 'How can Key Stage 2 SAT writing performance be improved? A study of high and low scoring papers', *Education 3–13* 29(3): 53–60.

Rheinberg, F., Vollmeyer, R. and Rollett, W. (2000) 'Motivation and action in self-regulated learning', in M. Boekhaerts, P.R. Pintrich and M. Zeidner (eds) *Handbook of Self-Regulation* (pp. 503–29), San Diego: Academic Press.

Rogoff, B. (1999) 'Cognitive development through social interaction: Vygotsky and Piaget', in P. Murphy (ed.) *Learners, Learning and Assessment*, London: PCP with OUP.

Sadler, D.R. (1989) 'Formative assessment and the design of instructional systems', *Instructional Science* 18(1): 119–44.

Sadler, D.R. (1998) 'Formative assessment: revisiting territory', *Assessment in Education* 5(1):77–84.

SCAA (Schools Curriculum and Assessment Authority) (1996) *Report on the 1995 Key Stage 2 Tests and Tasks in English, Mathematics and Science*, January, London: HMSO.

SCAA (1997) *Standards at Key Stage 2 English, Mathematics and Science: Report on the 1996 National Curriculum Assessment for 11-year-olds*, London: HMSO.

Schon, D.A. (1983) *The Reflective Practitioner*, New York: Basic Books.

Schools Examination and Assessment Council (1990) *Records of Achievement in Primary Schools*, London, HMSO.

Schratz, M. and Walker, R. (1995) *Research as Social Change*, London: Routledge.

Scriven, M. (1967) *The Methodology of Evaluation*, Washington DC: American Educational Research Association.

Silcock, P. (1999) *New Progressivism*, London: Falmer.

Simon, B. (1988) *Bending the Rules*, London: Lawrence & Wishort.

Skinner, B.F. (1968) *The Technology of Teaching*, New York: Appleton-Century-Crofts.

Skinner, B.F. (1969) *Contingencies of Reinforcement. A Theoretical Analysis*, New York: Appleton-Century-Crofts.

Stevenson, R. and Palmer, J. (1994) *Learning: Principles, Processes and Practices*, London: Cassell.

Tomlinson, J. (1989) 'Curriculum and the market: are they compatible?', in B. Moon *et al.* (eds) *Policies for the Curriculum*, London: Hodder & Stoughton.

Torrance, H. and Pryor, J. (1998) *Investigating Formative Assessment*, Milton Keynes: OUP.

Tunstall, P. and Gipps, C.V. (1996) 'How does your teacher help you make your work better? Children's understanding of formative assessment', *The Curriculum Journal* 7(2): 185–203.

Tyler, R.W. (1949) *Basic Principles of Curriculum and Instruction*, Chicago, IL: University of Chicago Press.

Valsiner, J. (1992) 'Social organisation of cognitive development', in A. Demitriou, M. Shayer and A.E. Efklides (eds) *Neo-Piagetian Theories of Cognitive Development: Implications and Applications for Education*, London: Routledge.

Vygotsky, L.S (1962) *Thought and Language*, Cambridge, MA: MIT Press.

Vygotsky, L.S. (1978) *Mind in Society: The Development of Higher Psychological Processes*, M. Cole, V. John-Steiner, S. Scribner and E. Souberman (eds), Cambridge, MA:Harvard University Press.

Wertsch, J.V. (1991) *Voices of the Mind*, London: Harvester/Wheatsheaf.

Wiliam, D. (2001) 'Reliability, validity and all that jazz', *Education 3–13* 29(3): 17–21.

Woodhead, C. (1995) 'Teaching quality: the issues and the evidence', in *Teaching Quality: The Primary Debate*, London: Ofsted.

Young, M.F.D. (1998) *The Curriculum of the Future*, London: Falmer.

Zimmerman, B.J. (2000) 'Attaining self-regulation', in M. Boekhaerts, P.R. Pintrich and M. Zeidner (eds) *Handbook of Self-Regulation* (pp. 13–39), San Diego: Academic Press.

Zimmerman, B.J. (1989) 'Models of self-regulated learning and academic achievement', in B.J. Zimmerman and D.H. Schunk (eds) (1989) *Self-*

Regulated Learning and Academic Achievement (pp. 1–24), New York: Springer-Verlag.

Zimmerman, B.J. and Schunk, D.H. (eds) (1989) *Self-Regulated Learning and Academic Achievement*, New York: Springer-Verlag.

Index